Praise for *The Fo*

"[A] clear-eyed and tender debut . . . [*The Forgotten Girls*] is as much the author's story as a piece of reportage."

—*The Wall Street Journal*

"Monica Potts returned to her hometown in Arkansas to figure out why so many of her peers were struggling. . . . Awash in research . . . Potts portrays Clinton in all its rugged beauty."

—*The New York Times Book Review*

"*The Forgotten Girls* is written without sentimentality, but it is elegiac all the same: a lament for lost opportunities and wasted lives; a controlled expression of rage at a system that continues to fail so many even as it exploits their despair."

—*The Guardian Observer*

"*The Forgotten Girls* rings with authenticity, a powerful, feminist, politics-made-personal analysis of how women in poor, white, religious societies suffer."

—*The Times*

"*The Forgotten Girls* is much more than a memoir; it's the unflinching story of rural women trying to live in the most rugged, ultra-religious and left-behind places in America. Rendering what she sees with poignancy and whip-smart analysis, Monica Potts took a gutsy, open-hearted journey home and turned it into art."

—Beth Macy, author of *Dopesick* and *Raising Lazarus*

"*The Forgotten Girls* is beautiful and hard, a deeply reported memoir of a place, a friendship, a childhood, and a country riven by systemic injustices transformed into individual tragedies. Monica Potts is a gifted writer; I read this extraordinary story of friendship and sisterhood, ambition and loss in rural America in one sitting. It is propulsive, clear, and really important."

—Rebecca Traister, author of *Good and Mad*

"A troubling tale of heartland America in cardiac arrest, of friendship tested, of meth and Sonic burgers and every other kind of bad nourishment, of what we have let happen to our rural towns, and what they have invited on themselves. A personal and highly readable story about two women in a small cranny of America, but which offers an illuminating panorama of where our country stands."

—Sam Quinones, author of *Dreamland* and *The Least of Us*

"A tender memoir of a lifelong friendship and a shocking account of hardship in rural America, *The Forgotten Girls* is beautifully written, painstakingly researched, and deeply affecting."

—Paula Hawkins, author of *The Girl on the Train*

"In a landscape where writing grounded in true events is expected to be either objective reporting about events from which the writer is fully detached or confessional lived experience, Monica Potts has created a rare mix of reportage and memoir that brings the best of both forms to bear on an empathetic and nuanced examination, told from an insider's perspective, of what it means to be working class, white, and female in America today."

—Emma Copley Eisenberg, author of *The Third Rainbow Girl*

"I couldn't put it down. . . . American culture has a toxic forgetting at its heart, a forgetting about communities that have lost their way and a blindness to why they fail. It made me think of so many people's lives in small towns and rural areas in Britain—a powerful reminder that when you forget about people and consign them to eternity in failing places, then you create something deeply harmful for all of us. It is an important book, raw and simple enough that you can't help but feel it deeply."
—James Rebanks, author of *The Shepherd's Life*

"A compelling sociological and cultural portrait that illuminates the silent hopelessness destroying not just [Potts's] hometown, but rural communities across America. A hauntingly cleareyed and poignant memoir with strong, illustrative reportage."
—*Kirkus Reviews* (starred review)

"A compassionate look at the rapid decline in life expectancy among 'the least educated white Americans' . . . Potts draws on extensive interviews with friends and family to reveal how poverty, generational trauma, substance abuse, and the suffocating righteousness of the evangelical church limit women's options in places like Clinton. . . . A potent study of what ails the depressed pockets of rural America."
—*Publishers Weekly*

THE
FORGOTTEN
GIRLS

THE
FORGOTTEN
GIRLS

A Memoir of Friendship
and Lost Promise in Rural America

Monica Potts

RANDOM HOUSE

NEW YORK

2024 Random House Trade Paperback Edition

Published in the United States by Random House, an imprint and division of
Penguin Random House LLC, New York.

RANDOM HOUSE and the HOUSE colophon are registered trademarks of
Penguin Random House LLC.

Originally published in hardcover in the United States by Random House,
an imprint and division of Penguin Random House LLC, in 2023.

Library of Congress Cataloging-in-Publication Data
Names: Potts, Monica, author.
Title: The forgotten girls / Monica Potts.
Description: New York: Random House, [2023]
Identifiers: LCCN 2022006767 (print) | LCCN 2022006768 (ebook) | ISBN
9780593730898 (hardcover) | ISBN 9780525519928 (ebook)
Subjects: LCSH: Potts, Monica. | Potts, Monica—Friends and associates. |
Women journalists—United States—Biography. | Female
friendship—Arkansas—Clinton. | Poor women—Arkansas—Clinton—Social
conditions. | Rural poor—Arkansas—Clinton—Social conditions. | Women
drug addicts—Arkansas—Clinton. | Arkansas—Biography.
Classification: LCC PN4874.P68 A3 2023 (print) | LCC PN4874.P68 (ebook) |
DDC 818/.603 [B]—dc23/eng/20230206
LC record available at https://lccn.loc.gov/2022006767
LC ebook record available at https://lccn.loc.gov/2022006768

ISBN 978-0-525-43536-5

Printed in the United States of America on acid-free paper

randomhousebooks.com

1st Printing

Book design by Diane Hobbing

For my mom

CONTENTS

AUTHOR'S NOTE

I began returning to Clinton and reporting for this book in the spring of 2015. I moved back during Christmas 2017, and from that time on, I was both a participant in and observer of everyday life here. I interviewed several friends and former classmates, especially Darci, who sat with me for hours, filling in her life's story. Most of our conversations were recorded. I read through thirteen of my childhood journal volumes, read Darci's diary, with her permission, and checked facts against public records and newspaper clippings whenever possible. At times, I had to rely on memory. At Darci's request, I changed the names of her children.

THE
FORGOTTEN
GIRLS

Prologue

One day when I was six, my parents hauled my two younger sisters and me around Van Buren County with a realtor, looking for a new house to rent. At the time, we lived in a run-down trailer in Shirley, Arkansas, but my parents wanted to move back to our hometown of Clinton—ten miles away, and at just over twenty-five hundred people, the biggest town in the area—where my dad wanted to start his own plumbing business. None of the places that we looked at were affordable for us, or if they were, they were not in livable condition. I have a sharp memory of my parents taking us gamely into the attic of a small house, promising it could be our bedroom and that we could climb the stairs every night on our own, only to find part of the roof missing and dead autumn leaves all over the floor. We bounced down unpaved rutted dirt roads and curvy country highways in our Ford LTD station wagon, up and down the hills, generously called mountains, that form the southern edge of the Ozarks. We trekked through mud and gravel and pine needles. My parents kept the search going all day even after it was clear nothing we saw would work.

Tired and cranky, I finally made it known that I was done. "I hate this town and I don't want to move!" I screamed. "And I hate all this nature!"

The realtor, whose cap of permed hair was shaped like a mushroom atop her head, looked back at me and cackled her smoker's laugh. "You'll think different someday."

That memory comes to mind every time I'm on top of Bee Branch Mountain, which crests just south of Clinton, my hometown. For twenty years as an adult, I lived elsewhere—going to college outside Philadelphia, and then living and working as a journalist in New York City, Stamford, Connecticut, and Washington, D.C. Whenever I came back for a visit, I had to drive over that mountain to get home from the airport in Little Rock. From its summit, I can see Van Buren County below me. Ahead of me the mountains stretch north, a mass of green hills that roll all the way up to the middle of Missouri.

My drive home had always been long and disorienting. Passing towns full of deprivation made me feel suffocated, as I had as a kid, and I felt pity for the people trapped there. But one day as I was driving home from the airport—I was older, in my thirties—I looked out from the the mountaintop, saw Clinton and the sparsely populated landscape beyond, and felt a flutter of homesickness. I've seen many landscapes that were objectively more beautiful: the man-made cityscapes of London and Paris and New York, the Atlantic and Pacific Oceans, the Mediterranean, the temperate rain forests of the Pacific Northwest. But none of those places were where I came from.

• • •

On Christmas Eve 2015, I was on Bee Branch Mountain again, this time looking for my childhood best friend, Darci Brawner.

Darci and I had reconnected eight months earlier, when she reached out to me through Facebook; before that, I'd seen her only once since high school, briefly, at my dad's funeral in November 2006. I'd been back in Clinton a number of times since we'd gotten back in touch, and we'd spent a lot of time together, catching up and getting to know each other again. Before flying in for Christmas, I had let her know I'd be in Clinton for the holiday, and she had asked me to drive her to Little Rock once I got there.

It was a long trip that I didn't want to make right after I got home, but I didn't know when I'd get another chance to see her. I warned Darci that I would need to get under way early in the morning so I could return to my mother's house by three p.m.—Momma needed her car for last-minute Christmas errands. I was also eager to have a nice dinner with my family—my mom, my sister, and my partner, Samir—who'd be waiting in the house for me to return.

When I set out to pick her up that morning, I followed the directions I'd scribbled in a reporter's notebook. I followed them south on the highway and then up Bee Branch Mountain. Across from the flooded old rock quarry where we used to go swimming, where minerals turned the water sapphire blue, I turned onto a little dirt road. I hoped Google Maps would help me navigate the rest of the way.

Darci was staying with a man named James, but she hadn't seemed entirely sure where he lived, even as she tried to explain it to me. "On paper," she kept saying, sounding drunk. "I'm only staying at that address on paper. Do you understand?" I didn't.

The road at the top of the mountain, rocky and heavily rutted, looked as though it hadn't been graded in decades. If I'd met another car coming the other direction, I would have had to pull over into the ditch to let it pass. Knee-high, weedy grass lined the edges of the road, and brown vines covered the barren trees like a wintry jungle. I got no cell reception, and my Google Maps app gave me up for lost. I could only surmise from the mailboxes that someone lived back here. I pushed forward, despite my fear of damaging the two-year-old Buick SUV I'd just helped my mom buy. It wasn't fit for such a road.

The first house I saw, James's father's, was a double-wide trailer, blue with neat trim. Behind it was James's little single-wide. It was small and weather-beaten, with corrugated metal walls that would not resist a strong wind, and like so many trailers in the area, it had a wooden porch and a wood-frame exoskeleton, all working together to prop it up. Four dogs ran up to greet my car, and when they wouldn't move, I parked along the road, far from the house. Getting out, I was thankful I'd worn my boots and old yoga pants, which I didn't mind getting dirty. There was a camper off to the side, beneath a garage-size wooden shed, and muddy yard. Two lawn chairs had been set up around a meat smoker that smelled of chicken. A path of stones led me to the trailer.

A man I took to be James opened the door. He was a couple of inches taller than my own five foot five, thin and wiry, with the kind of tanned, rough skin white people get after years of outside work, and a mop of dirty blond hair. He was wearing a Budweiser T-shirt and holding a Budweiser can. "Are you Darci's friend?" he asked. "She should be ready any minute." He turned, and I followed him inside.

The trailer was gloomy, with dark, fake-wood-paneled walls and too few windows curtained with dark sheets. It had a kitchen on one end, with cabinets of particleboard and laminate and a little kitchen island stacked with papers and food and beer.

The living room was big enough only for a couch and a TV. A Great Dane–size mutt lifted its head in excitement. A man who was older than James, with pale skin, dark hair, and a moustache, was sitting there, and I introduced myself.

"Was Billy Potts your daddy?" he asked.

I said yes.

He looked at me with eyes that were watery from beer. "I knew him. He was a good man." Both he and James were working on the forty-eight pack on the counter.

Darci emerged from the only bedroom, holding a mason jar

that smelled strongly of apple wine. "Give me a minute, I just need to find my makeup bag." She brushed her fingers through her curly black hair.

She had been straightening her hair since we were kids, but now she seemed to be getting the job only half done: she'd pulled it back into a headband, but pieces kept popping out like unruly twigs. She wore wide, flowing multicolored, multipatterned pants and a tank top. Her voice was raspy, her speech punctuated with quick staccato laughs. She'd always liked to laugh and to make people laugh and often wore half a smirk, as if she were entertained by the world. Whenever I saw her, it felt like we'd never stopped knowing each other.

I followed her into the small bedroom and sat down on the edge of the bed. She kept turning around, forgetting from one minute to the next what she was doing. Pieces of hair would pop up; she'd smooth them down, then put on makeup, then look for something, over and over again.

The dogs tumbled into the bedroom, and I patted them while fending off offers for beer from the men. "We need to get on the road," I nudged, and we finally made it out of the bedroom.

Darci stuffed her cigarettes and lighter into her purse, set down her mason jar, and went up to James, who was pulling food out of a decrepit fridge. "I need some money," she said bluntly. He gave her a twenty, and she gave him a kiss.

Darci and James had met only weeks before. Before staying at his place, I'd later learn, she'd had no income and had been homeless. Was her need for shelter the reason for the relationship? I would ask her later, and she said no. But in the past, when she'd needed places to stay, or money, or security, she'd always relied on relationships with men. This was my first view into how unstable her life had become.

"I'm sorry if I smell like alcohol," she said shakily from the passenger seat, as we buckled up. "My throat was hurting so bad. . . . These are some of the best people." She indicated the trailer through the windshield. "They'll do anything nice for me, but they're stern."

I was distracted backing out of the yard and dodging the dogs, so I didn't ask what she meant by *stern*. Most of her conversation, as we drove away, was incoherent rambling that went nowhere except unrelated tendrils of conversation.

"How do you know James?" I asked.

"That's where it gets crazy is right there with James," she said. "Oh my gosh, Monica, you wouldn't believe the things that go on in these hills. I look around, and I'm like, 'Is this really happening?'"

. . .

When Darci contacted me out of the blue, I knew only that our lives had gone in radically different directions. I had become a journalist, and I'd been returning to my hometown in the mountains to investigate a disturbing trend. A team of University of Illinois Chicago population health experts led by Jay Olshansky (in a study published in *Health Affairs* in August 2012) had found that white women who did not graduate from high school were dying five years younger than such women had a generation before. For their male counterparts, it was three years.

Study after study over the next decade supported that initial overall finding: the least educated white Americans were dying younger than they had in the previous generation. Such a rapid drop in life expectancy almost never happens absent war, an earth-shattering political revolution, or a global pandemic. Two of these things would come later: the political upheaval manifested in Donald Trump's election and augmented by his tenure as president, and the devastation wrought by Covid-19 in 2020. But the drop began before those events.

That the decline was among white Americans surprised everyone, including me. Black Americans in general have higher rates of mortality than whites at every age, as a result of systemic racism, prejudice, and uneven medical care. But the racial gap in mortality had been targeted for change, and it had been closing, albeit too slowly, so that at least before the Covid-19 pandemic hit, Black Americans were living longer. But even as the racial gap closed, the drop in life expectancy among white Americans showed that the education gap was widening.

From 2014 to 2017, the decline in life expectancy among the least educated white Americans, women in particular, was the longest and most sustained in a hundred years, according to the *Journal of the American Medical Association*. In 2015 Anne Case and Angus Deaton, economists at Princeton University, found that the drop in life expectancy, especially for middle-aged whites, was largely attributable to increases in drug overdoses, suicides, and complications from alcoholism, a trio of ailments they called "deaths of despair." As Case and Deaton continued their work in the following years, they found these deaths were equally distributed between white men and women in this group; they discounted deaths from smoking, a habit that had persisted for the least educated white women even as it had decreased for other groups.

Diseases of despair weren't the only reason these women were dying. In 2018 two economists at Dartmouth College, Paul Novosad and Charlie Rafkin, found that deaths from all causes, not just deaths of despair, were rising among the least educated whites. "The least educated middle-aged white women, in particular, are now at higher risk of dying from cancer, heart diseases and respiratory diseases, among other causes, even as mortality from these causes has declined sharply for those outside of the bottom 10 percent," they wrote.* This group seemed to be suffering from a range of disadvantages, and the complexity of the issues made it difficult for researchers to identify a specific cause for this trend. "It's hard to point out this one specific variable that's driven this increase in mortality," Rafkin told me. "It's that there's this general malaise."

Words like *malaise* and *despair* hint at stories that can't be told with data and statistics. This, I felt, was where the work of sociologists and economists and public health experts ended and my work as a journalist began. The kinds of deaths the researchers had noticed were increasing more for some people than for others, and in some places more than in others. So I decided to return to my Ozark hometown, with its aging, shrinking population, governed by a small group of people who worshipped at the same churches as their parents and who had knit around themselves an ever thicker and tighter web of personal and political self-deceits.

Even as the Covid-19 pandemic hit, these long-term trends continued. When the virus first arrived in the United States, it affected people in the Northeast and people of color the hardest. Mortality spiked by 23 percent overall: white Americans lost an average of 1.36 years of life, Black Americans lost 3.25 years, and Latinos lost 3.88 years. Once vaccines became universally available, however, the death rates for many groups dropped. But for middle-aged, white Americans in rural areas like my hometown, they rose. In the last half of 2021, this was attributable largely to persistent vaccine hesitancy, especially among white evangelical Republicans, which the Public Religion Research Institute found to be the most vaccine-hesitant group in the country. Even into 2022,

---

* They looked at a slightly differently population, which included some high school graduates who hadn't gone on to college, and found a slightly smaller three-year decline in life expectancy for white women in this group.

less than half of the population of Clinton was fully vaccinated. And as the Delta and Omicron variants spread, people died despite the availability of free vaccines that could have saved nearly all of them. Still raging, underneath the virus, were the opioid and meth epidemics, made worse by the isolation and uncertainty wrought by the pandemic, and from the rise of fentanyl, a more deadly synthetic opioid that replaced drugs like OxyContin and heroin in the illegal supply because it was cheaper and easier to obtain.

When I started looking into why less educated, rural white women were dying and what was killing them, I thought my investigation would be straightforward. Study after study had offered answers: methamphetamines, opiates, suicide, and smoking. And yet each of these taken alone was unsatisfactory. Why did a drug like meth take over in some places but not others? Why would prescription painkillers, which are available everywhere, kill poor, uneducated white people in greater numbers than other groups? Why did the rate of suicide rise and spread in rural areas faster than elsewhere? Why did some women persist in smoking even though everyone knows it's disastrous to health? None of these questions had simple answers, but trying to answer all of them would take me past research and into the circumstances, accidents, and personal choices that fill and shape our lives.

I thought I was looking for the women most affected by these changes, those most in danger of dying: What was different about their lives and why? It turned out, though, that I was looking for only one person.

For many years, I had avoided Darci on purpose. When I'd left home at eighteen, she'd been kicked out of high school weeks before graduation, or at least that was how I'd remembered it. Before I left for college, we'd said goodbye at a funeral, a painful capstone to an often painful childhood. I was eager to leave, to close the book on Clinton and the people in it. Thereafter, as I built my life elsewhere, I tried not to think about what I'd left behind, what life was like for the people I loved. I sensed, from little things I heard, that Darci's life had not gone as she'd hoped. When I finally did go back, I realized that my investigation would turn on all the questions science couldn't answer, on what my best friend's life had been like after I'd left, and on how she'd ended up in that trailer on top of the mountain.

. . .

When we reconnected in April 2015, Darci had insisted on taking a photo. It shows us with our arms around each other, leaning in. I'm smiling big, wearing lipstick, in a summer dress and light jacket, and looking confidently into the camera. Darci is wearing her flowy, floral clothes with headbands pulling back her hair, and she grins the easy smile of someone who loves to have her photo taken. In the years that followed, she insisted on taking a picture of us nearly every time we met. Over the years, my smiles fade until they're nonexistent, and we hold each other a little less close each time. The pictures become less frequent, because Darci was fading away from me again.

When I began my investigation into what was happening to women like Darci, I didn't realize how personal and emotional this journey would become, that it would take me through layers of long-buried grief and the pain of watching a loved one fall apart. Instead, as I set out, my plan was first to remember how Darci and I had lived as children, when both our young lives had held so much promise. Then I would retrace all that had happened in the years after I left and she stayed, mapping the steps that had taken us further apart. I would find the answers to all my questions in the space that had grown between us.

Part I

Causes

1.

Place

When I left Clinton for college at eighteen, I thought I'd never come back. My mom, Kathy, had always lived in terror that her daughters would get stuck in Clinton, so for most of my life, I knew I would leave and stay gone. Fear propelled me outward, dominating my relationship to my hometown as I grew up.

When I was twenty-four, in 2004, my dad, Billy, was diagnosed with lung cancer. He was given less than two years to live, but he responded well to treatment. Two years later, in the summer of 2006, the cancer had gotten so small that doctors couldn't detect it on scans. That was what my sister Courtney and I were told. Courtney was living in Denver, and I was in New York.

Then in the fall of 2006, his cancer came back suddenly and fiercely, leading to a two-week hospital stay. My mom didn't tell us. My dad was released from the hospital, but he was so weak that my mom and her friend had to help him up the stairs. They still didn't tell Courtney or me how ill he'd become. I was working at *The New York Times* as a news assistant and had vacation days that I needed to use before the end of the year, so I could have gone home, and if I had, I would have been with them during his last week. Instead, I stayed in New York, having dinners and drinks with friends, spending long days at museums, relaxing. I think about that week a lot, imagining my dad stumbling into his bedroom for the last time.

A few days after he came home from the hospital, Daddy was watching the TV show *Lost* when he called downstairs to my mom and said something weird: "Doesn't that actress look like her grandfather?" Momma rushed upstairs and found him seizing. He was rushed to the hospital again, for what proved to be the last time. Finally, Momma called us. By the time Courtney and I flew home, our father was in the Veterans Administration hospital in Little Rock, receiving treatment. Tumors covered his brain, and the doctors said they could do nothing but make him comfortable in his last days.

He couldn't talk to us, just made a whispery *whir whir whir* sound. We saw in his eyes, though, that he was trying to communicate something. We struggled to decipher it. Was he trying to tell Momma to take care of his dog, Puppy? we asked. He nodded and sighed with the most relieved look I've ever seen. We hugged him, and he combed his fingers through our hair, as he'd done when we were little. He was fifty-five. We'd always known that Daddy, a heavy smoker and drinker, would die young. He'd known it too.

Courtney and I stayed as long as we could but then had to return to our respective cities. He died soon afterward, and we flew back to bury him. The last time I'd been inside the town's United Methodist church, I'd attended someone else's funeral. Mourning him in the same place now felt like closing a grim, traumatic loop.

I'm not sure I've ever forgiven Momma for not telling us before it was too late. "Your daddy didn't want you girls to know," she said during our first fight about it. "We were afraid you'd quit your jobs and rush home." For years afterward, whenever someone else died, or when Puppy died—which she told me about very casually in a text message—I'd call her up and yell at her, angry and accusatory. I'd ask her again what I'd asked her then—"Why on earth would we have quit our jobs and come back?"—and she'd just say she didn't know. But her fear was so deep and irrational that she thought we would lose the opportunities that leaving had afforded us simply by coming home. She couldn't imagine a world in which we had stable lives while also staying connected to our family.

She had actually gotten out once. After high school, she'd lived for a few struggling years in and around Chicago. She had moved back after a personal trauma that she told us about only when we were grown. So our being able to live elsewhere felt momentous to her. It had taken so much effort on her part to ensure that we left, and then she worried that she would ruin it for us, that some family trauma would force us to return, as she had had to return. So she hid the struggles of people in Clinton from us. She was proud that Courtney and I didn't live in Clinton, but her pride came at a cost: I'd missed that last week with my dad, and I often felt a little unmoored and displaced, as if I had no home at all.

• • •

As I moved about the world as an adult, it was rare for me to meet someone from Arkansas, let alone from the Ozarks. People frequently told me I was the first person they'd ever met from the state. It's an odd, sparsely populated place. The Ozark Plateau, which straddles the northern half of Arkansas and the southern half of Missouri, was carved into hills and modest mountains by rivers and creeks that still trickle eastward, joining up with bigger streams until they run into the Mississippi. The town of Clinton, located just north of Bee Branch Mountain on the southern edge of the range, lies in a wide valley where two big creeks come together in a Y. Whenever I journey down into the valley and toward town, it feels like the mountains are folding in to envelop me; and whenever I leave, I have to climb a mountain again.

Long ago the Osage, among others, used the bluffs as shelters, but people who arrived later came and went with the seasons, using the lands more as hunting grounds than for cultivation. White settlement forced Native Americans away from the territory, west into Oklahoma—the Trail of Tears passed through Arkansas. European immigrants trickled in slowly, never in large numbers, and they tried to force the hills to become farmland. The first surveys, starting about 1819, show roughly a dozen homesteaders living in what would become Van Buren County. Some of the areas north of us were even less populated. Settlement hardly sped up even when Arkansas became a state, in 1836. Van Buren County covers 724 square miles, about twice the area as the five boroughs of New York, but today the city has almost five hundred times as many people—eight million compared to just under seventeen thousand. Even when I lived in New York and traveled regularly back and forth, it was almost impossible to wrap my head around the difference in scale and density.

Once they arrived, settlers with English, Scottish, and Irish names lived in the river valleys, which flooded regularly. Once those lands were taken, all that was left were the rocky hilltops. The interplay of mountain and water, and the problems it could cause, defined the rhythm of life and made it difficult to succeed as a farmer on the slopes. Most of the mountain's inhabitants were subsistence farmers, poor by the old definition of the word: they could not feed their families. This pattern was repeated through most of rural America: white settlers came from elsewhere and tried to impose their old crops and ways of life onto the new landscape.

The project was doomed from the start. In an 1878 report, John Wesley Powell, the soldier and geologist who served as the second head of the U.S. Geological Survey, warned that most of the lands west of the Mississippi were unsuitable for farming. Even the

Great Plains, which seemed rich and fertile, were in reality mostly arid and semi-arid. Yet the federal government still promoted the idea of the rugged individual farmer-settler, insisting that any American could be successful through sheer force of effort.

Trying to bend the continent to our will was arrogant, and it did not work. American society left people to find prosperity where it couldn't be found; when they didn't, the country did little for them. The flip side of American independence is a tendency to abandon people to their fates. Today parts of rural America are diverse and vibrant, but most people in rural counties in the middle of the country are older, whiter, less educated, and more conservative than the nation as a whole. They're also suffering economically and losing population, and the women are dying younger. If you compare the statistics of drug use and increasing mortality in rural America with a map of the United States, you'll see the geography of places where, generations ago, people were set up for failure.*

* As defined by the U.S. Department of Agriculture's Health Resources and Services Administration, an area is rural based on its population and its distance from a city of at least 50,000 residents. The United States has 3,100 counties (or similarly sized political entities), and by the definition used by the rural health service, 2,243, or 75 percent of them, are considered rural to varying degrees. Van Buren County, with a population of less than 17,000 and shrinking, is in the most rural category. Rural counties encompass the vast majority of the physical land in the United States, but they hold only about 20 percent of the nation's population. Rural counties are not identical. In 2019 the American Communities Project, based at Georgetown University, set out to understand them in all their diversity. They're not all white—some 370 rural counties have a substantial Black population, and 43 have large Native American populations. Another handful, about 161, have large and growing Latino populations, driven largely by migration from Central and South America. In some of those counties, white non-Hispanics are now the minority. The vast majority of rural counties, however, are whiter and slightly older than the rest of the U.S. population. In the median rural county, the population is 78 percent white and more than 20 percent of the population is 65 or older, compared with national averages of about 61 percent and 16 percent, respectively.

A popular myth persists, in Southern counties like mine, that the people in the mountains were too poor to own slaves. White Southerners repeat this point often to try to absolve themselves from the guilt of slavery, but it's only partly true. From 1830 to 1860, slaves made up just under 4 percent of Van Buren County's small population, similar to the percentage in other highland areas. In 1860 two hundred enslaved people lived here, in an overall county population of 5,357; throughout Arkansas, about a quarter of white families owned slaves. Their unpaid labor built the state. Most of the rocky land remained unwanted and unsettled even after the Civil War, when the Homestead Act finally included newly freed Black Americans, but some freedmen did come to northern Arkansas to make claims. They fled worse conditions farther east, where slavery had technically ended but had continued in spirit through sharecropping and forced labor. Around 1900 two Black communities were formed on the southern boundary of Van Buren County, centered on two African American Baptist churches: Solomon Grove and Zion Grove.

Albessie Thompson, a local historian of the present-day town of Twin Groves who helped found its library, told me that a group of whites came down from the hills to burn the church and the schoolhouse in Solomon Grove some time after they were founded. In response, Solomon Grove relocated to join its sister community at Zion Grove, on higher land, forming Twin Groves. Driving African Americans from good farmland with violence was a common practice both during and after Reconstruction. This pattern would repeat over the years, so that small, isolated white communities like the one I grew up in stayed that way, closing themselves off, especially to newcomers who did not look like them. The state's schools were officially integrated in 1972, four years after my mom finished high school, but before then the Ozarks' Black students were bused to Faulkner County. The Ozarks themselves were home to isolated hate groups advertising hostility to anyone but white Protestants with familiar English, Scottish, and Irish surnames.

For more than one hundred years, from their early settlement until the end of World War II, the populations of these counties, including Van Buren, stayed in the low thousands, and families lived on small farms where they survived on what little they grew. Deprivation showed itself in grim statistics: infant mortality was and remains highest in rural counties, and three-quarters of the U.S. counties with the highest rates of hunger were and still are in rural areas. The federal government didn't measure or track poverty officially until the Johnson administration's Great Society legislation of 1964. The first official numbers came out in 1980. Poverty in rural America afflicted 17.5 percent of its population, compared to 12.9 percent in cities, and in some counties it was three times what it was in urban areas. The rate of poverty for Black Americans, at 32.5 percent, was higher than for whites overall.* But most of the nation's poor whites lived in counties like mine. How well they fared depended on how good their farms were, and around my hometown, the farms weren't very good.

Van Buren County "is probably to the state of Arkansas what Arkansas is to the rest of the United States—a great paradox—to some a rare jewel among an assortment of worthless rocks, while to others a few crumbs from the table of a great feast," Jim Duncan wrote in a chapter of *The History of Van Buren County*, a book compiled in 1976 by civic-minded residents for the U.S. Bicentennial. It was one of my favorite books to flip through as a kid, giving me new insight into the familiar landscape of my home. Downtown Clinton wraps around a two-story courthouse

---

* Today the poverty rate for Black Americans remains above the national average, at 22 percent.

with native stone siding, built in 1934 with money from the Works Progress Administration, and buildings of brick and stone with big windows front the square. While I was growing up, Clinton's downtown was falling into disrepair, with busted sidewalks and empty lots. But the pictures in the book showed the courthouse square as the center of a vibrant frontier life, full of local groceries, hardware stores, and banks; on weekends, locals put on their nice clothes and filled the square for town dances. That kind of communal life continued into my mom's teenage years.

Two decades after Jim Duncan wrote that book, he was my high school history teacher. He'd begun teaching at Clinton High during my mom's final year, 1968. By the time I knew him, he had a mop of gray hair and metal-framed glasses. He always chewed a toothpick and kept it clenched tightly in his mouth. He gave a pop quiz at the start of every class, mostly to ensure that we'd done the reading, barking out ten questions, leaning back in his chair so that his cowboy boots poked out from under the desk. The quizzes gave him a reputation for toughness, but students liked him anyway. Mr. Duncan died in 2015, but I didn't find out until a couple of years later, and I was sad I hadn't had the chance to mourn him.

"Rich land and better economic opportunities," he wrote in the book, "were usually the two main reasons for people moving into the west during the 1800s. Admittedly, Van Buren County didn't offer an abundance of either. Where one may find beauty and great delight another may grope for morsels of happiness finding only despair."

I can almost hear his clear, southern-accented voice as I read this section. In it, he seems to be wondering why people want to live here at all. Continuing to move west was the story of America, he wrote. Some would move farther west, to better opportunities. When my mom's dad, Joseph, was thirteen during the

Great Depression, he moved with his family to California's Central Valley, like a protagonist in a Steinbeck novel. There he met and married my grandmother, Aurora, daughter of Portuguese immigrants. He saved the money he made picking oranges and working at a cannery so that he could buy back his family's hundred-acre plot in Arkansas, which had been lost to the bank when they couldn't make the mortgage.

This story sounded almost too novelistic for me to believe, until as an adult, I found the birth certificates and land records confirming it. My grandfather's sisters stayed in California, and I had two glamorous great-aunts who visited every few years. His notion as a young man was purely a sentimental one: he'd wanted to own the land his father and grandfather had farmed, and he was too poor to own farmland in California. It had been so romantic, he convinced my grandmother to come back with him, leaving me, their granddaughter, to yearn for the dream life I might have had in California. His American desire to own land was so powerful that he had given up prosperity elsewhere to do it.

Why did anyone stay in Van Buren County, or even come back, like my grandpa did? I'm sure the answer, for many people, was the availability and cheapness of the land. For others, the beautiful mountains made it possible to ignore the hardships. For others still, the hills offered escape from a society that mistreated them, or didn't value their work, or had once enslaved them. Once they chose to stay, leaving was difficult, and not just for poverty or other logistical reasons. It was hard to imagine going somewhere new and unfamiliar, and in such an isolated place, everywhere else was unfamiliar. Leaving the comforts of home, however meager, and the slow, easy rhythms of life there takes a longing imagination and an all-consuming drive, like my mom's. But these qualities also made her unwilling to tell her daughters when their father was dying, so they were a mixed blessing.

. . .

Momma grew up on the land her father had bought back from the bank, just south of downtown Clinton. Her family called it, somewhat ambitiously, "the Farm," though it had never grown more than cabbages and corn for them to eat, and a little bit of hay for my grandfather to sell to more prosperous farmers. Both her parents worked at the local chicken-processing plant until they retired, earning just enough to support their five children.

Momma was the oldest, born in 1950. She had two outfits, she used to tell me when I'd beg for new clothes, and she had to wash them out and hang them to dry every night—white shirts with stains in the armpits, and woolen skirts she had to wear even in the suffocating humidity and heat of the Arkansas summer. She had to change her siblings' diapers and help shuck corn, but she had nothing else to do, no books or magazines to read. She told me this whenever I complained about having to do any chore.

As a teenager in the mid-1960s, she took a job at the Ozark Café, which everyone called the Bus Stop, because it was where the buses stopped on their way to and from town. It was on U.S. Highway 65, which at that time cut through downtown Clinton— the federal government was still building the national highway system that was meant to connect even the remotest parts of the nation. She saved her money and bought new clothes and candy bars for her siblings and herself. She told me about that whenever I fought with my two younger sisters so that I would act like the bigger person and be more generous and we'd all get along.

My mom was smart and beautiful, tall at five foot seven with olive skin and bright black eyes and black hair that she kept curled and short, teased high atop her head. Family pictures of her and her sisters taken in the 1960s and '70s, on the porch at their old house, show them in ratty old T-shirts and cutoff jean shorts that looked stylish on their slim figures: they looked like an old ad with glamorously shabby hippie models. If my mom had grown up in California, I thought, she would have gone to college and marched braless through the campus or on a city street as part of the feminist movement. Instead, she was a poor farm girl. She did not go to college or march for anything.

She did go to Chicago, right after her last year of high school, in 1968, and stayed until 1976. She rarely talked about it, but she let stuff leak out occasionally. She worked at a restaurant where she learned to make twice-baked potatoes, and she'd make them for us for dinner sometimes. She worked as a waitress and steered clear of handsy old men. When we watched the Kirstie Alley movie *A Bunny's Tale*, about Gloria Steinem's investigation of the Playboy Club, Momma said she'd been to the one in Chicago once. She kept a big wooden chest at the foot of her bed. When I asked about it, she'd just say, "That's from Illinois," and I'd know to leave it at that.

Daddy's family was poorer than my mom's. Billy, my dad, was the youngest of six: three boys who had red hair like their mom, and three girls who had black hair like their dad. When they were kids, the family moved north to Indiana, where his parents worked as farm laborers. They were alcoholics, and in the black and white pictures from this time, they look like honky-tonkers up to no good: my biological grandfather, Jess, was always smirking, and my grandmother, Nadene, whom I called Mammaw, was stony-faced. My dad used to tell me—casually, the way people do when they don't realize that what they're saying is heartbreakingly sad—about the time his next-oldest brother, my uncle Roy, stabbed him for a piece of chicken, and how he and Roy used to steal milk bottles from their neighbors' porches, and about the feasts that they'd have whenever money came because they'd gone hungry in the weeks leading up to its arrival.

When my dad was about thirteen, Mammaw quit drinking, divorced Jess, and moved back to Clinton, where she married another man who lived in town. Daddy came with her, and in the years that followed, all but one of his siblings trickled down to join them. Daddy became estranged from his biological father, who soon moved back to live on his family's wooded, wild, unfarmed land on the mountain north of town. The mountain itself was casually called a racial epithet when I was growing up. I can't find any record of how it came to be called that, but several friends who moved through Clinton during their childhoods, living here only for a short time, told me they heard the N-word used on the school playground in Clinton more than they did anywhere else in their lives, thrown around with abandon. In polite company, people called the mountain north of town simply the Mountain. The Mountain was always connected, for me, with my dad's sprawling, confusing family, stretching over several generations and down several dirt roads. There were generations of cousins named Potts, Bigelow, and Willoughby, several of whom I did not realize I was related to until I was much older, many of them men who drank with Daddy, many of them often in trouble with the law.

I called my stepgrandfather, Gene Starcher, Pappaw, even though he and Mammaw had divorced by the time I knew them. Pappaw and Daddy were close. Daddy had enlisted in the army in 1973, because—again, uttered very casually—"war was better than home." The Vietnam War ended before he made it there. Afterward he picked up odd jobs, like chasing chickens for farmers before sale day, until Pappaw, who was a plumber, invited Billy and his brothers to apprentice with him. "I think Gene Starcher saved your daddy," Momma used to say. "If not for Pappaw, Daddy would have been even more of a drunk."

My parents met after my mom returned to Arkansas and her friend, Johnnie Ruth, convinced her to play on a softball team that her husband, Nolan, coached. Nolan was Daddy's brother, and Daddy was always around, too, teasing Momma and Johnnie Ruth from the sidelines while they stood in the outfield, smoking, talking, and being really bad at softball. The four of them became friends, and Momma and Daddy started dating. My parents lived together—"in sin and degradation," they used to joke—until the spring of 1977, when they married.

For their wedding, Momma wore a long, elegant, light-blue dress with a halter top and empire waist. Daddy wore a blue suit with a red striped tie, his bright red hair catching the sun, his smile big under his moustache. She was twenty-seven, and he was twenty-six. "Your momma robbed the cradle when she snagged me," Daddy used to joke. They were both so good-looking then, with high cheekbones and fit bodies that did not wear their hardships yet. The family wedding was in the yard of the Farm, with tall, yellow broom sedge grasses growing wild around them. In the photos, my mom's dark-haired family, huddled around in their farm clothes, look like old-world peasants, while Mammaw and Pappaw stand by Daddy, Mammaw grim-faced as usual.

• • •

When I was born at the end of 1979, people thought Van Buren County was on the way up. Throughout rural America, the federal government had pumped in money to build new highways, dam rivers for flood control, and increase the number of homeowners through subsidized mortgages. These policies were largely limited to white families, and they helped lift many out of poverty. Three branches of the Little Red River, including the two that met in Clinton and troubled the town with floodwaters, the Archey Fork and the South Fork, were dammed to help build a lake straddling this county and the next one, called Greers Ferry Lake. All this meant new jobs for people in construction like my dad and other dads I knew, who worked for highway departments and water departments or as plumbers and builders.

The lake brought with it the promise of tourism and recreational jobs and money, in addition to the hydroelectric power that would help finally connect the rural outreaches to the electric grid. A group of developers bought thousands of acres of old farmland near the lake and began building housing and condominium units for a planned retirement community called Fairfield Bay, hoping that bringing in retired residents who had pensions and didn't need jobs would increase the county's fortunes, a strategy for rural counties across the United States. The work of building up the county gave men like my dad steady work for much of my early childhood.

My sister Ashley was born sixteen months after me. In those years, we moved from one old rented home to another. The first one I remember was a small blue square house on the Mountain that had belonged to my uncle Nolan and aunt Johnnie Ruth, the couple who had introduced my parents. But my uncle and aunt had separated by then, after Uncle Nolan had an affair. The man whose wife he slept with shot and killed him during a poker game, in March 1980, when I was about five months old. In gloomy, drunken moments throughout my childhood, Daddy would tell me how happy Uncle Nolan had been that Daddy had had a daughter.

When Daddy got a job with a construction company in Fairfield Bay, we moved to an old brown and tan trailer on a highway in Shirley, a town even smaller than Clinton, about ten miles northeast of it, with only three hundred people. I don't remember much of these early years, except what I've filled in from photos: Ashley and I are in diapers and pigtails in a grassy field, blowing dandelions or standing in our underwear posing in sunglasses;

I'm wearing my mom's, perched upside down on my nose, arms crossed, trying to be glamorous, while Ashley, barely a toddler, stands straight-armed beside me, her mouth open, giving a confused look to the camera, wearing a jumper and pink Porky Pig sunglasses with one lens missing.

My mom continued to work after I was born, and one of my dad's cousins, who ran a daycare service in her home, minded us during the day. Like many moms we knew, she did the largest share of parental work by far. It was too much to handle while she was working too. She'd wake early in the morning, get us dressed, and get us to daycare. The county unemployment agency, where she worked, had been consolidated with Faulkner County farther south, so she had to drive for more than an hour down twisty, narrow mountain roads to the college town of Conway. She quit soon after.

Later, when we couldn't have something we wanted because we didn't have the money, we would ask her why she no longer worked like some other moms we knew. She would tell us about the story of the day she decided to quit: "I sat up one morning, and I was already in the parking lot at work. And I had no memory of how I got there. I thought, 'If I stay in this job, I'm going to die.'"

The decision to leave work seemed even more justified when Momma had Courtney when I was five and Ashley was four. Momma stayed at home, in the trailer, raising her three girls, because the cost of daycare and gas would have taken up most of her salary. But what she said, and what a 2016 Pew Research Center survey shows a majority of Americans still believe, was that children were better off with one parent, usually their moms, staying at home with them, even if it meant relying only on the man's unsteady pay. It dropped our family of five below the poverty line.

With Momma at home taking care of us and no reason to go

anywhere, we were insular and a little lonely. We didn't have neighbors or sidewalks like they did on *Sesame Street*. The houses we lived in didn't look like those we saw on television, so they seemed unreal. Without neighborhood kids to play with, Ashley and I played with each other. We both had dark, almost black hair, so straight it wouldn't even hold a braid, and in the summer we'd run around outside without any sunscreen and get tanned, our faces splashed with freckles. I had my mom's square jaw, wide nose, and big forehead. As I grew, I would continue to look just like my mother: we even had the same crooked front tooth. Ashley was fairer, and her features more delicate, with a turned-up nose for mischief, and an elfin, pixie lightness to her, thin as a twig. I would always be a chubby kid, and heavy in another way, too, more down to earth, more grounded. I was a rule follower, compliant; I wanted adults to pat me on the head and say "good girl." Ashley's shyness tended toward stubbornness, and people had country nicknames for her. She was a ring-tailed tooter. Momma called her a piss-ant.

When we each turned three, Momma enrolled us in dance school. For toddlers, dance just meant wearing stiff ruffles and tapping our feet to songs like Stephen Sondheim's "Broadway Baby":

I'm just a Broadway Baby.
Walking off my tired feet.
Pounding Forty-second Street
To be in a show.

The year Ashley was four, her class was doing a dance she thought was stupid, and she refused to practice. She swore she'd refuse to do it in the recital too. And there she stood at showtime, stiff-armed through the whole performance. Oddly, she kept hitting her marks; when the line of girls moved up, she moved up with them, and when they moved back, she'd glance over and walk back with them, maintaining the jagged row of curly-haired, lipsticked toddlers. She just refused to do the moves. The VHS recording caught all the adults laughing.

"Ugh, Ashley, you're so stupid!" I said when she joined me backstage. I turned from her and crossed my arms, refusing to speak to her for the rest of the show. I never would have dared to do that; I anticipated what adults wanted from me. Ashley couldn't be made to do anything. I resented her for it even as she was annoyed with me for caring so much about rules and what people thought.

If our lives together were a coloring book, my pages were always colored inside the lines, with every shade chosen for perfectly logical reasons; hers were covered with dark, intense, waxy crayon, colors chosen without regard for how they compared with the real world. In the years since, every piece of literature, every movie, every real-life story has confirmed for me what I learned then: that no two people were ever more different, or more inseparable, than sisters close in age. We fused together then, especially in the years before Courtney was old enough to really play with us. The Potts girls. A unit. And that's how people thought of us too.

• • •

I went through Head Start, kindergarten, and half of first grade in Shirley. During that Christmas break, in the winter of 1986–87, my family moved back to Clinton. We found a small yellow-brick house downtown, behind the post office, just off the courthouse square. Rent was $250 a month. Four years earlier, nine feet of water had flooded the square after a series of winter rains saturated the ground and raised the rivers. The courthouse square was the town's business district, and many of the storefronts had flooded and were still empty when we moved back. The main highway, U.S. 65, was rebuilt on higher land to bypass downtown. More businesses would leave during my childhood and teenage years, and downtown would keep dying.

Our house was one of the last few in the floodplain. Early every morning, from our big living room windows, we saw the mail carriers load up their trucks at the post office, and we watched lawyers and accountants and hairdressers and clothing store owners pass by, and we eventually walked the few blocks to the dance school by ourselves. But we were still lonely kids. Looking back, I realize how exquisitely alone my mom was, too, even in town. She sat on the couch, looking out the windows, smoking and reading a book most of the hours we were at school and often when we were home. She was a reluctant housewife and did not enjoy cooking or cleaning or, I think, childrearing. Our loud little lives filled the house, and I didn't notice, as a child, how depressed Momma must have been. Especially because Daddy was never there.

My dad had completed enough hours to get his master plumber's license, and he opened his business: Potts Plumbing Company. He printed up a bunch of T-shirts showing an old country man sitting in an outhouse, with the slogan IN OUR BUSINESS, A FLUSH IS BETTER THAN A FULL HOUSE. He printed up pens and passed them around. He advertised at the grocery stores, the Piggly Wiggly and Thriftway. He explained the joke to everyone, laughing his wheezy, contagious laugh through his dentures, which he wore most of my childhood. Daddy was looking a little rough by then, in his midthirties; his skin was too red from working in the sun, and his belly was starting to swell from too much beer. But we felt we were moving up.

I didn't know anyone at school except Ashley, but she was a grade below me and didn't share a recess with the first and second grades. So one day when I was in first grade, during recess, I was watching the boys kick a rubber ball down the slope of a rocky hill. It dropped quickly, and dangerously, down to a busy road where trucks hauled chickens to the nearby processing plant where my grandparents worked. Sometimes the boys would curl up into balls and roll straight down. Adults were around, but we played like that, careless and carefree, without a word of warning from them. Sometimes we led expeditions down the back of the playground toward the muddy banks of the busy, rushing South Fork River, and no one missed us. That was life in Clinton.

While I watched, a girl in my class named Tara came up to me and said, "Darci wants to know if you're from China."

"What?" I said nervously. I was wearing my favorite purple sweater, my hair pulled back in a ponytail.

Darci bounded over to me. Her curly black hair framed her face. Her skin was pale and freckled, like mine and my sisters', but her face was marshmallowy and doughy, with a smirky smile and bright, mischievous black eyes. Her face made her seem soft, but her spirit was all sharp-elbowed energy, and she looked straight at me as she asked, "Are you from China? I've never seen someone with such straight black hair."

No one of East Asian descent lived in our overwhelmingly white town, but she was eager to meet me, not to make fun. Faced with such a brave, curious, and adventurous girl, I could do nothing but befriend her.

Darci and I were the special kind of friends who spent our free time together even during years when we didn't share a classroom. As a child, I didn't think about the ways our families were similar and different. But her parents, like mine, were working class and had not gone to college. She and I both received free school lunches and government boxes of food but were shielded from the worst parts of poverty. Both our dads were blue-collar breadwinners, and both our moms left the workforce when we were young, although once Darci was in school, her mom, Virginia, got a job as a secretary at a water utility company.

Both sets of parents, for most of that time, were together. Many of our friends came from divorced households and spent weekends at their dads' houses—so we rarely met their dads. Darci's dad, Dennis, worked at the chicken-processing plant at night, so he was often on his way out the door when we got home from school. That's generally how I thought of dads then: distant, rarely seen figures, away at work or absent altogether. It was the moms who ran the sleepovers. Virginia and my mom were friendly. When one of our moms dropped us off or picked us up at the other's house, they'd linger and chat. They'd known each other in high school, although Virginia was a couple of years younger than Momma. The two women sometimes walked together for exercise. Both were avid readers, especially of mysteries and romances. They'd trade library books when they finished them and before the two-week loan period was up so they didn't have to wait to get their hands on new releases. The similarities between our parents gave both Darci and me a sense of familiarity; our houses felt comfortable, unintimidating, and safe.

Virginia wore her light brown hair short. It curled around her face, although it was less curly than Darci's. Her skin too was pale and clear, and her loud, bouncy nasal laugh sounded almost like the words in a children's book: "HA-HA-HA." She seemed a little less sour than my mom, slightly happier. When she came home from work, she rushed into the kitchen, still wearing her work slacks and sandals, to cook supper, just like my mom did the minute we got off the bus. But sometimes Dennis would come through the kitchen on his way to work, while Virginia was making Mexican Chicken Casserole or scalloped potatoes, and pretend to start to tickle her; she laughed her ha-ha laugh before he even touched her. They seemed more intimate than my parents. There was always something wholesome and a little soft about Virginia, warm and inviting. But maybe she was too tender, melting into laughter before actually being tickled, unable to withstand the forces that would come her way.

Darci's brother, Cody, was three years older than us. They were close, but it wasn't the same as having sisters. Darci came over to our downtown house more often than I went to hers, and she played with my sisters as well as me. Momma remembers that Darci entered our world of make-believe eagerly, as if she were hungry for it. Ashley would come up with elaborate skits and characters. "I'm Merocono!" she'd say, in an exaggerated old-man accent. Merocono was her made-up character; she'd pop up in front of us, wearing a white wool cap from deep in the closet, sporting a stick as a cane. She'd fill the sink with water and dishwashing liquid for the bubbles and then pat the bubbles around her chin to make a beard. Merocono was, for some reason, an old schoolteacher, and we'd sit at some old wooden desks we had and patiently listen while Merocono lectured to us.

Not many girls would have jumped so wholly into our weird games, especially Ashley's. But Darci tried to match her energy. She once convinced us that she talked in her sleep, but during one slumber party, she blurted out, "I'm Popeye, the sailor man!" from under her blankets, and we knew she was just trying to trick us. She tried to convince us she was a sleepwalker, too, and one night we found her walking stiff-legged in a hallway, but then she burst out laughing and gave the game away. Darci could say "Where's the beef!?!" just like the lady in the Wendy's commercials. She could sing the popular country song "Swingin'" and gave impromptu performances, uncharacteristically timid but clear, in the middle of our living room: "We was swingin', just a swingin'." We put on dramatic living room productions of Winnie-the-Pooh stories: *Winnie-the-Pooh and the Blustery Day* was a favorite. I normally played Pooh, but when Darci was around, I was Owl or Eeyore. Ashley always chose Tigger, which fit her boundless energy, and Courtney, the youngest and smallest, had to play Piglet whether she wanted to or not.

We'd go into the bathroom to make magic potions, stirring shampoos and conditioners into gloopy messes that we left for Momma to clean up. We'd spend long hours outside, exploring our muddy yard and trying to excavate diamonds. Behind the house was a worn dirt path, and if we looked at it from a certain angle, we could imagine it actually led somewhere.

Darci was between Ashley and me in age but also in personality. Like me, she was serious and studious in school. We were in the Gifted and Talented class together. When we had to design a biographical diorama of our favorite author's life, I was mad at Darci for snagging Judy Blume first. She won first place for her project, and I won second. Later, in eighth grade, when we had to write a short story based on a picture pulled, without context, from a magazine, I won first place and Darci second. Every year the finalists for the Newbery Award for children's literature lined our school library's shelves, and we read those books voraciously. They took us to exotic places—in *Tallahassee Higgins,* a girl's mother went to Hollywood and left her with an aunt and uncle in Maryland, and *Island of the Blue Dolphins* and *I Heard the Owl Call My Name* took us to the Pacific coast. One year Darci found Judy Blume's *Forever,* about a teenage girl's sexual adventures with her boyfriend, and during our library hour we flipped through to the romantic parts. Darci was my only friend who read as quickly and widely as I did, and it set us apart in our friend circle.

Like Ashley, Darci had a creative, energetic, independent streak, but she didn't have Ashley's troubles in school. Ashley was quiet most of the time but was prone to loud outbursts and laughing fits. She often got into trouble for not being able to sit still in her seat. She came home with notes from teachers, and Momma and sometimes even Daddy trudged over to the school for conferences with her teachers.

Darci hated Clinton, or at least she was willing to imagine a life elsewhere. We spent long hours in my room looking at an old world atlas, tan with brown binding. We'd flip through states and look at the cities, labeled in bold. We skipped the ones that seemed too big, like New York and Los Angeles—even in our daydreams, we couldn't wrap our heads around them. Instead, we'd trace the boundaries of the more manageable towns—Fairfax, Virginia; Tucson, Arizona—picturing living there without knowing much about them. We imagined they had rows and rows of two-story houses on roads with street signs and sidewalks, which our town did not have. We dreamed of living as neighbors in adobe houses in New Mexico. Maybe we could live in a town that had a public pool, or in one with snow in the winter, like Burlington, Vermont.

In fourth grade, I made it onto the Quiz Bowl team, a kind of trivia tournament. That Friday at recess, I started to tell my friends I wouldn't be in school the following Thursday. Darci jumped in and said, "She's moving to Fresno, California."

Fresno was one of our towns. Darci's eyes sparkled, and her smile set into a smirk.

I ran with the joke. "Yeah," I said, "y'all will never see me again."

"Why are you moving?" Tara asked.

"Daddy got a job," I said casually.

"Yeah," Darci said. "At least one of us gets to leave Arkansas."

Darci and I broke out in giggles, unable to keep up the joke. Fresno had an exciting, bold name. It didn't matter what the city was really like—it had to be better than here. And I'd always felt I had a parallel dream life there, the one I might have had if my grandparents hadn't moved back to Arkansas.

None of the other girls laughed or cared or understood. The dream of moving to California was Darci's and mine, and we kept it alive through the years. When we entered high school, in 1994, we decided that for our senior trip, we would drive to California, our gift to ourselves for graduating. We bought a road atlas and mapped out the journey, taking side roads through the desert, making stops along historic Route 66. I imagined us as tall and skinny teenagers, wearing clothes like we saw in *Sassy* and *YM*, baby doll dresses with Doc Martens. We'd take a break, then enroll in some faraway college to study English and become writers. We'd listen to Janis Joplin and rap and alt-rock—which none of our radio stations played—and finally get out.

• • •

In my thirties, when I started going back to Clinton for visits, I would linger and work remotely, enjoying my stays. During one of my trips, I found the childhood journals I'd kept from fourth grade, in 1989, through most of college, ending in 2001, filling most of thirteen books in total. I was surprised, reading them as an adult, to see how much my attitude toward my hometown mirrored my mom's. In the summer of 1991, at twelve, I was already desperate to move. "I want to see new people and new places," I wrote in my journal. "I want to move to any state besides Oklahoma or Mississippi. I found out that out of all three, Arkansas is the best of the worst." In December 1994, moody over a boyfriend, I wrote: "I hate this town. I hate everyone in it. Everything in my life is wrong."

Why had Momma never left Clinton? I wondered. She could have moved away after Courtney and I left home, after Daddy died. Instead, she stayed and kept hating it, complaining about it.

When Daddy got sick, my parents had barely survived on his Social Security disability. They fell into poverty and declared bankruptcy. Momma eventually found a job in the financial office of the local hospital, and she continued to work there through her sixties and into her seventies. She'd come home from work, feed her dogs, then sit on her couch with her e-reader or phone in her hand. She'd read or play solitaire or Candy Crush, the games *ping-ping-ping*ing while the phone cast a soft glow on her face, still framed by her short black hair, which she kept dyed and curled. She only ever looked up to complain, like about traffic: "These women here, they drive these big trucks, and you can tell they don't know how to handle them. They're going to cause an accident." *Ping ping ping.* Sometimes she'd complain that no one she knew traveled, that they enjoyed being isolated and closed off from the world. "A friend from work said, 'Kathy, I have no desire to see the world, or have it come to us,' and I'll say, 'Well, the world's going to intrude into your little bubble whether you like it or not.' " *Ping ping ping.*

While Barack Obama was president, Clinton was full of birthers, people who continued to insist the president was born in Kenya despite all evidence to the contrary. A co-worker sent Momma a racist email of a watermelon patch taking up the White House Rose Garden, and Momma said, "I mean, the woman who sent it to me has a Black grandchild!" It was an old Southerner's mistake, I thought, to expect that familial love would prevent racism. When Donald Trump ran for president and then won in 2016, support for him raged in our hometown, combining two things that tormented my mother: conservative politics and evangelical religion. "This freaking nightmare is never going to end," she would wail. The people she worked with would huddle together and talk about Trump's presidency being ordained, especially after he moved the U.S. embassy in Israel to Jerusalem, a provocative change that fundamentalist Christians thought would hasten the end days. "They say we are going to destruct from within," my mother said, throwing her hands into the air. "My question is, what does that have to do with anything? What does this have to do with the rapture?!?"

Momma didn't just complain to me; she also said what she thought about the town to her neighbors and friends. What people said about my mom in return was that she was blunt. Some people thought her rude, or, in their nicer moments, honest. I came to understand why Momma was so ready to disapprove, and why she shared her disapproval. She used to say that Southern women dripped honey when they spoke. They maintained a strict politeness on the surface, unwilling to criticize or complain, smoothing over disagreements before they could turn into arguments. But these small-town niceties often masked cruelties and injustices. Momma wanted to puncture that with realistic assessments, to point out what was wrong and what was right. I came to be that way, too, and sometimes found myself more openly judgmental in my hometown than anywhere else, feeling an urge to puncture the superficial sense of accord.

After Daddy died, Momma's own health suffered in small and big ways, the result of age and years of heavy smoking. My biggest worry was that she wouldn't tell me if she got sick, the way she'd kept Daddy's final illness from us. I desperately wanted her to live a good, healthy, long life, as some of my friends' parents did, but I feared she wouldn't. Two of her siblings had died before they turned fifty. On my dad's side, none of his siblings had lived to see seventy, and two of them had died before forty. The studies I read, showing that white Americans were losing life expectancy at a rapid clip, were alarming, but then, I'd always known that life was harder and shorter for some than for others.

2.

Church

The differences between my family and Darci's became more obvious to me as I grew older, and the biggest difference was that Virginia was very religious, like most of the women in town. Momma, a lapsed Catholic, was not. She grudgingly took us to the United Methodist Church when Ashley and I—Courtney was still a baby—begged to go because we were the only children we knew who didn't go to a church. For most of her life, Virginia had attended the Seventh-day Adventist church in town. This evangelical denomination met on Saturday mornings, which seemed to me like the worst of all worlds: Darci always missed Saturday-morning cartoons. Later, I learned that the early Seventh-day Adventists organized their doctrine around the apocalyptic books of the Bible; their foundational belief was that the world would soon end and that believers would be called to heaven while sinners remained trapped on earth. They were not the only Christians in town to have a strain of apocalyptic thinking; in some ways, Christians have been waiting two thousand years for the world to end.

Most of the kids I knew spent their summers attending Bible schools with friends and families in their own churches. Darci and I did too. Virginia played the piano and ran the vacation Bible school at her church, and I used to go with Darci. At the last meeting of the weeklong day camp, Virginia would give a quiet, timid speech to the kids. "What was your favorite part?" she'd ask. And we'd all say "Arts and crafts!" And she'd repeat, "Arts and crafts?" as if it were a question, and laugh.

Some of Darci's friends at church had Old Testament names, like Esther and Micah, and some of the girls wore long skirts. Darci went every Saturday and attended youth group events around the state, but she was never, as my friends and I would say, a Holy Roller, she wasn't part of the long-skirt-and-bun crew, like the most religious people in our school, the Pentecostals.

At school, children and teachers spoke about church frequently. Prayer was omnipresent. The population was overwhelmingly evangelical and Protestant. *Evangelical* is a word that's often misunderstood—it refers to an eighteenth-century movement within Protestantism that put first the belief that salvation comes through God's word as given to us in the Bible. From this premise stemmed the beliefs and practices that set evangelicals apart from other Christians—the idea that one can be "born again," the importance of having a personal relationship with God, and the driving need to spread God's word to others. As I was growing up in an evangelical culture, people spoke about their version of Christianity, it seemed, everywhere and all the time. Worship was incorporated into classrooms and workspaces in a heavy, omnipresent way. We prayed before football games, and my fellow students talked about being saved. Later, as teenage girls, being Christian determined how we did or didn't act. Evangelical Christianity is conservative and authoritarian, and I didn't like it. It led me to suspect religion in general and to believe that Christianity was constraining and antiwoman. I came to this worldview early, and since then, the way I've seen evangelical Christians interact with the world at large and in national politics has mostly confirmed those impressions.

The biggest religious group in Clinton, and in the South as a whole, were the Southern Baptists. The Southern Baptist Convention is a loose affiliation of churches—there's no hierarchy—that formed in 1845 after they split off from national Baptist groups because of the rising antislavery sentiment among the Northerners. Southern Baptists continued to support slavery throughout the Civil War and later defended segregation, a stance they finally apologized for in 1995. In 2018 the denomination's largest seminary, in Greenville, South Carolina, apologized because its four founders had owned slaves. Because the Southern Baptists don't have archbishops commanding from on high, their philosophy can vary from congregation to congregation, but the churches are steeped in the old Southern aristocracy: traditional, conservative, and white, with men at the top.

The Southern Baptist Convention is one of the largest evangelical associations in the country. The Association of Religious Data Archives (ARDA), a kind of religious census, shows that in the 1980s and '90s, when Darci and I were growing up, at least half the population of Van Buren County attended church regularly. The biggest group by far were evangelical Christians, at 83 percent of all regular churchgoers. Within that group, 64 percent were part of a Southern Baptist Convention congregation, and there were three more Baptist churches that weren't specifically Southern Baptist. There was only one mainline Protestant denomination in the whole county, the United Methodist Church, which had congregations in Clinton and in other towns. A mere 140 Catholics attended mass in two parishes, making theirs the most exotic church I knew about growing up. There was no data on any non-Christian religious groups in Van Buren or many other Ozark counties.

The numbers are similar across the American South today. In Van Buren County, 4,017 of the 7,057 regular churchgoers attend one of the eighteen Southern Baptist congregations, the largest single group by far, followed by the Churches of Christ, another evangelical congregation. Nondenominational evangelical churches have seen a rise in rural areas, but these congregations are not tracked by ARDA. The religiosity, and the conservative religious beliefs, are pervasive. And if you were to place a map of white evangelical Protestants over maps of women dying young and overdosing on drugs and going without jobs, they'd line up. Poor white people with the least education, who live in areas with high concentrations of evangelical Protestants, are the ones who are dying young. Case and Deaton, in their 2020 book, *Deaths of Despair and the Future of Capitalism,* noted this correlation and said that while religion could have a positive effect on the life and well-being of individual people, "religious *places*—including U.S. states—do worse on the same outcomes. Religion helps people do better, and they espouse religion in part *because* their local environment is difficult."

Not even these high numbers for church attendance convey how powerful conservative religion is in these areas. Churches hold services on Sunday mornings, Sunday nights, and Wednesday nights. In an isolated small town without much entertainment, they host activities for teenagers and children and social gatherings throughout the year. When I was growing up, Bible school was our summer camp. A few churches welcomed nonmembers to their events, but people generally went to their own churches and organized their social lives around them. People at lower income levels couldn't always afford the gas to drive into town or the nice Sunday clothes that many of our churches required, so attending church every week in person was more difficult for them. As a result, more people identified as Christian than attended church weekly.

On one of my visits home, I met up with a local friend, April

Burris, who'd lived away from Arkansas for seven years, on Long Island. But when keeping up with rent became too overwhelming, she decided to move home. She is now agnostic. As a child and a teenager, she'd attended an Assembly of God church, which is a less strict Pentecostal faith, then later switched to First Baptist because popular kids went there. She went primarily to socialize, she told me.

First Baptist Church is a brick building with a big, flashing electronic sign in front, on the new Highway 65. After a flood in 1982, businesses left Clinton's downtown, draining the courthouse square of the vibrant civic life people had enjoyed in the 1960s and '70s. First Baptist filled the vacuum. In the 1980s, its congregation boomed, growing to nearly a thousand. As it grew, it had more money to spend and expanded, building playgrounds for children and participating in activities around the country. Eventually it would build its own preschool.

While I was growing up, power radiated from First Baptist Church, and the pressure to conform to its standards was enormous. April remembered that as a child, she was taught at church how to be a lady. Ladies crossed their legs so that boys couldn't see up their dresses. Ladies were quiet and polite. Ladies didn't ask too many questions, and they certainly didn't raise a fuss. Posters with inspirational quotes lined the walls: A WOMAN WILL WIN HER HUSBAND OVER WITH A GENTLE AND QUIET SPIRIT. Girls got in trouble for any transgression. "Boys could get by with anything," April remembered, "but girls were held to a higher standard."

As we got older, the messaging became more direct. "I remember sitting around in metal chairs," April told me, "and hearing how we needed to keep ourselves pure for our husbands, and all the things we would have to do to be their helpmeets." While April was in college, barely out of her teens, a Baptist counselor and minister advised her to stay with an abusive boyfriend. She was supposed to pray for him. Once at First Baptist Church, a youth pastor confessed to infidelity, and his wife was called to stand in front of the entire congregation and forgive him. "Everything was, 'What can you do to be a better wife for your husband?'" April remembered.

Men gave the sermons on Sundays and led the congregations publicly, while women led behind the scenes, doing the hard work of running logistics for every food pantry, coat drive, or spaghetti dinner fundraiser. The church set girls up to be of service to everyone and in charge of nothing.

Many evangelical Christians view their religious mission as outward facing: they believe the world around them should reflect their values, and they try to influence the world according to those values. This kind of biblically based activism—using the Gospel for social reform—is part of the way the National Association of Evangelicals, a pan-denominational association of churches, defines evangelicalism. God is everywhere, in football games, in public schools, and in state and local governments.

While evangelical churches around the country were building political influence and working harder to affect state and national politics, in small towns their power was already complete, and they used it. Male leaders of the churches are elected to, or get appointed to, leadership positions in their towns and counties. The mayors, the representatives on county governing bodies, the quorum courts, the sheriffs, are mostly people who belong to the big churches. When I was in high school, three of five members of the school board attended First Baptist Church. These officials were almost always male: Southern Baptists generally do not believe women can be leaders. Once men are in authority, they are part of God's authority: whatever they do becomes part of God's plan. For those in power, this has the benefit of preventing constituents from questioning their governance.

In 1998, after I graduated from high school, a relatively new young teacher named Kim Trujillo assigned her seventh-grade English class to read *Summer of My German Soldier*, written by an Arkansas author, Bette Greene. During World War II, rural Arkansas had been home both to a Japanese internment camp and to a German prisoner-of-war camp; the book was a fictional account based on the latter. Because of the book's roots in the state, Arkansas schools commonly taught it. Mrs. Trujillo adopted it because the previous English teacher had it in her curriculum, and the students read it in her class for her first three years at the school.

But that year a woman who attended First Baptist Church, whose son was in the class, flipped through the book and found the phrase *God damn* in it three times. Rather than go directly to Mrs. Trujillo to complain, which would have been the norm, this mother went to the school superintendent, Curtis Turner, who also attended First Baptist Church and was in only his second year in that position. "I don't know why, but he went into a rampage," Mrs. Trujillo told me. "He wanted to take out every book in the entire school system that had any bad words in it."

A censorship drive brewed inside First Baptist Church. "I don't want my children to read anything with profane language," Turner told a columnist for the state newspaper. "That's my own religious conviction and stance." The school board called an unscheduled meeting to determine whether all books with curse words should be pulled from school libraries, or perhaps those words should be inked out. Mrs. Trujillo became the center of the controversy: people came up to her in her own church, a Church of Christ, to ask her why she would teach such blasphemy. She was scared she'd lose her job. (She didn't.)

Today the book is controversial across the country. It's about a young girl's romance, and some find it sexually suggestive. It illustrates the racism and anti-Semitism endemic in the South in the 1940s. For English teachers, those issues offer opportunities for education. "We couldn't even get the parents to read the book to show them that it's a worthwhile book that has good lessons that are worthwhile about history," Mrs. Trujillo told me.

Other teachers rallied around Mrs. Trujillo, including some of the teachers who attended First Baptist Church. If the school board banned the word *damn*, Shakespeare's *Macbeth* would also fail to pass their censorship test. It was a rare moment when the church was divided, and for once the women banded together and successfully influenced the men on the school board, which voted 3 to 2 not to censor all the books in the school.

Away at Bryn Mawr, I watched the fight from afar and found it embarrassing more than anything else. Those driving for censorship said they were worried about the welfare of the students, but I agreed with Mrs. Trujillo's feeling that "they were trying to make this big Christian statement, making them look like they were being really strong Christians by going after someone who was allowing such smut." The biggest church in town didn't care that Mrs. Trujillo was also a Christian. Having the new superintendent as one of its members, First Baptist was flexing its muscles, showing where the power lay. I think it was also trying to put a new, young teacher in her place a bit. Mrs. Trujillo didn't teach that book again.

In 2000, soon after I left, white evangelicals succeeded in influencing national politics with the election of George W. Bush as U.S. president. People who aren't from the Bible Belt often confuse the Christian values on which these voters based their political choices with a notion of personal piety. But when evangelical voters talk about values, they mean public values, not their personal relationship with Jesus. According to Christian values, a public school should ban all the books with naughty words in them, because if you believe God would object to those books, then no one should read them.* This is how religion becomes less a personal belief system than a tool for social control.

Promoting Christian values, in this sense, involves using your influence to spread what you believe about God. That's why, even though my sisters and I never attended an evangelical church, the values of the biggest churches in town affected our childhoods. And we were exposed to their teaching that the proper role of women and girls was to live under male authority.

When I revisited Clinton as an adult, I traveled around the churches on Sundays. At almost every one of them, I heard, at least once, a lesson about the need to trust fully in God's plan, to give one's life up to God. Common, too, was a theme of turning to God in times of trouble and asking God for help. I never heard, in church or elsewhere, a group of people sit down and say, *Okay now, how do we solve this problem?* People went to churches that preached heaven as the ultimate reward for people who were personally pious and Christian and repentant; earth was just a temporary place. "For this world is not our permanent home; we are looking forward to a home yet to come," reads Hebrews 13:14, or as translated more clearly in a popular hymn: "This World Is Not My Home." If that's the case, why struggle to make the world better? Better to concentrate on one's faith. This philosophy conveniently absolves people who are better off—financially and materially—from trying to help those in need: the despair unfolding around them is part of God's plan, and the responsibility to escape into heaven belongs to each individual person.

* Polling bears this out. In 2015 the Barna Group, a research organization that studies Christian trends, asked evangelicals why they voted the way they did, and 58 percent of those who responded said that a candidate's stance on issues mattered most. Fewer than half answered that they cared most about a candidate's personal character or religious faith.

In the summer of 2018, I went to my first Southern Baptist Sunday school class as an adult. I got there early and found the parking lot mostly empty. I didn't realize it, but the church was just overcoming a tumultuous period: its previous pastor had resigned after having an affair with a married congregant, announcing from the pulpit that he didn't feel he'd been leading a Christian life and that he had to step down from his role.

From the parking lot, I followed another couple into the adult Sunday school room, cozy with wood paneling and carpet, and sat down on one of the big plush couches that lined the walls.

The teacher that day was one of my high school friends' dads, Jim Evans. "Today we're going to talk about the benefits of submitting to authority," he said to the dozen or so adults who had piled in around me. "What are the benefits to human authority being limited?" he asked.

"It should force us to rely on God," someone said. "It should make us want to rely on God."

The thoughts continued: It was important to trust blindly in God, to fully submit to God's plan. Without God's authority, we all lived in chaos. It should be a relief to be able to rely on God and not to worry so much.

"God already has our stories written," said a woman wearing a long T-shirt dress, with a tattoo on her ankle. "We can't change it. God's authority is supreme."

Another woman piped up that for women, it was especially important to learn to live under someone else's authority, like that of her husband.

I realized I'd been picking up on this message throughout my life, although I'd never heard it so clearly and explicitly stated. Women could go only as far as they could influence the men around them to take them. The message enforced a strict gender division: men and women had natural, God-given roles that were fundamentally different. It expressed a worldview that didn't allow for gender fluidity, for recognizing trans and nonbinary lives.

These attitudes seem old, as if rural Arkansas had been untouched by the rights revolutions of the mid- to late twentieth century, but they arose in reaction against the women's liberation movement and books like Betty Friedan's *The Feminine Mystique*. To counter feminist rhetoric, both male and female evangelical teachers asserted that the only thing that makes women truly happy is submission to their husbands and to the natural order. Straying from that ideal is the cause of every unhappiness. Marie Griffith, a religious scholar at Washington University in St. Louis, has found that evangelical women's groups explicitly tell a woman that if her husband, or some other male authority figure, is making her unhappy, all she needs to do is pray and return to the Lord, and then she will find that her husband has been a loving, good man all along and that her unhappiness was all in her own head. "Family harmony," she observes, "hinges upon the expectation that each member will perform his or her God-ordained role properly, accepting and following its prescriptions."

For women, that means submitting both to the church and to their husbands, and that "pain may be healed through a submissive and disciplined commitment to what is perceived as true Christian womanhood." More broadly, it means that women are to endure suffering, not solve it or complain about it. It sets up a woman's role as one of constant sacrifice and martyrdom. Religious communities intend for women to pray for everything, not to have the power to make decisions for themselves or for their communities.

Momma rejected this religious worldview, and as I read my journal as an adult, I was surprised at how quickly and thoroughly I absorbed it too. In one passage, I wrote about how Darci and I were obsessed with the boy band New Kids on the Block. (So were many girls our age.) For my eleventh birthday in 1990, my parents bought tickets for their upcoming concert in Little Rock. Momma had enough funds on her credit card to buy tickets for herself, Ashley, Courtney, and me, and for each of us to bring one friend. I brought Darci.

Darci, Ashley, and I piled into the back of our minivan, while Courtney, Ashley's friend, and Courtney's friend squeezed into the middle, barely fitting into a seat meant for two. Daddy drove the hour-and-a-half trip, and we were uncontainably excited. Darci and I argued over who liked New Kids on the Block better. We accused each other of being fakers and competed to see who knew more about them.

"What religion do you think the New Kids are?" Darci asked.

"Catholic, I think," I said.

"Why?"

"Because Joey McIntyre went to a private Catholic school," I said, "and was taught by nuns."

"I guess we can assume they all are, then," she said. "That's called drawing conclusions. I think most people in Boston are Catholic because of who settled there. The Irish. Like the Celtics, which my brother likes."

"Actually, I'm pretty sure the pilgrims in Plymouth were something with a *P,* like Purists."

We paused and looked out the window, getting close to the city.

"Everyone around here is Baptist," Darci said.

"I know. I hate it. Baptists are so stupid," I said. "Remember when the First Baptists tried to save us at their vacation Bible school?"

During an afternoon assembly, the pastor had asked us to come up to the front of the chapel, if we were ready, and accept Jesus into our hearts, a common ritual in evangelical churches.

"I know, I got sooooo mad," Darci said. "Half the kids went to other churches."

Momma turned around. "Baptists in the North believe a lot different from Baptists down here."

I got passionate. "I'll move out of the South before I have kids, because people around here are so stupid! I'll probably get married in Boston because I want to go to Harvard."

"Monica"—Darci rolled her eyes—"do you really think you're going to get to go to Harvard?"

"I doubt it." I sighed. "But if you're going to dream, why not dream big?"

Maybe it started then, with little differences, slight turns in the trajectory that pushed us further apart as we aged. When Virginia started going to Baptist churches, she took Darci with her. When troubles hit, they turned to these churches, where they prayed and trusted in God's plan. Once, as an adult, I asked Virginia what she did when she was stressed out or worried. "Oh you know, I just give it up to God," she told me. Virginia was happy in Arkansas. She wanted the life the church promised her, and she tried to get it. She had thought that if she followed a life of order and authority, good things would unfold. When they didn't, there was nothing she could do about it but pray. Darci had always been more exposed to, even saturated in, this type of religiosity than I had been. Her life might not have seemed God-fearing to an outsider, but in her bleakest moments, her faith in God's plan was what she relied on—and it almost always let her down.

3.

The School Hill House

I often struggle to remember Darci as she was as a child. I carried the fact of her being my childhood best friend throughout my life, like a keepsake. It felt like she had always been there in the background, and when I try to bring to mind our childhood and teenage years together there is an overwhelming sense of warmth and friendship, but also one of loss because the memories are fading.

Pages of my journals mention Darci at a regular clip, but without specifics because I didn't need them. I took her for granted, the way sisters take each other for granted. "Darci's coming over later," I'd note. "Talked to Darci." We spoke on the phone for hours. "You two would call just to update each other on how many times you went to the bathroom," Momma used to say, annoyed that we were tying up the line for hours on evenings and weekends.

It's hard to fathom what we talked about so endlessly, and I'm not even sure teenage girls still do that in the era of texting. "I just went over to Darci's house and I had fun," I wrote in my journal in the winter of 1994. "I always have fun at her house and she never gets on my nerves because she's smart and she's not a stupid girl."

Darci was a less faithful, less avid diarist than I was, but she did keep a small diary—in a pink and green plastic cover, decorated with hearts and bows—from 1989 to 1992. Years later, with her permission, I read it. I was relieved to discover that she'd felt the same. "At Monica's last birthday party we got into a fight and I mean really a fight," she wrote in November 1991, when I'd just turned twelve. "We weren't friends at all for a week and a half. But now we're great friends again and I'm really glad!!!"

In 1990, Darci and her family had moved from the modest A-frame house that she'd lived in since I met her to a slightly bigger house across from the high school. All of Clinton's public schools—elementary, middle, and high—are near each other in a loose, sprawling collection of tidy brick buildings that start on top of a hill, called School Hill, next to the downtown and slope down the backside until the entire campus ends in a rodeo arena, a baseball and softball park, and the chicken-processing plant. Behind it all, the milky green South Fork river runs on its way to meet the Archey Fork river south of the downtown and on to the lake. In any given year, roughly twelve hundred students, from Clinton and from smaller communities around the county, fill the classrooms. The total students in kindergarten through twelfth grade barely fill one slim yearbook.

The part of School Hill that faces downtown rises so steeply that it forms a cliff along the old highway. In spring, spontaneous waterfalls pour over the edge to the ditch by the roadside; in summer, tangled green weeds cling to the tightly pancaked layers of rock; in winter, the waterfalls turn to ice as if they were frozen midflow. When I was young, this made me feel like I was entering Narnia. Because School Hill is elevated from the floodplain, it is one of the town's oldest, most densely populated areas, with neat, older clapboard and brick houses. Some of the richest families once lived there. The schools keep the neighborhood busy and vibrant, the heartbeat of a town that doesn't have much going on for adults and therefore revolves around its kids.

Today the school campuses are fenced off and access to them is controlled, but in my day we had the run of School Hill on weekends and throughout the summer. We'd play on the playgrounds and walk past the empty buildings, which took on a spooky quality when school was out. We shared the road to the chicken-processing plant with chicken trucks, the smell of fowl and guts and chickenshit permeating our memories. The plant closed in 2008, its empty hulking buildings and silos of beige concrete and rusting steel feel post-apocalyptic. A single guard posted in a shed at the gate now makes sure no one vandalizes the place.

My most vibrant memories are from middle school. Between the ages of ten and fourteen, we played and enjoyed school and life in a relatively carefree way. Ashley, despite being a year younger than me, shifted to spending more time with Courtney, even though she was four years younger than her and still in elementary school. This alliance allowed Ashley to hold on to her childhood a bit longer. Courtney was the shyest of us, painfully so during her early years. In middle school, as Ashley's peers became interested in clothes and makeup and boyfriends, they teased her for her tomboyish, playful ways. Together my sisters found solace in the world they continued to create for themselves. Courtney would do anything Ashley said, a willing lackey and production assistant. They still played characters and staged theater productions. With an old VHS recorder someone had given us, they made a series of movies called *Adventures in Kittens,* starring our poor, unspayed Mittens's new litters.

Darci and I, more independent now, found new ways to engage with the world, through movies and TV, and *Sassy* and *YM* and *Seventeen* magazines, and books. Darci knew a girl from her summer church camp—a slightly older teenager with impeccable skin and nice clothes from the mall—who lived in Little Rock. Darci visited on weekends and would bring back VHS recordings of MTV, episodes of *Beavis and Butthead*, and concerts like Nirvana on *MTV Unplugged*.

Darci's parents' house on School Hill had a large den separate from the rest of the house, with its own entrance and exit. Her parents couldn't hear us from their room and almost never intruded. We'd watch the tapes for hours, stretched out on her house's old shag carpet. Our interests were ours alone: everyone around us listened to country music and knew nothing about the shows we were watching. It really hit us then how isolated Clinton was, how different it was from the worlds onscreen that we were exploring from afar. It reaffirmed our desire to get out.

Our sporty teenage peers wore simple T-shirts or polo shirts and jeans, with socks and sneakers. The other big clique wore Wranglers and cowboy boots. I wanted to wear baby-doll dresses, chokers, and combat boots. "I like grungier, hippie-type clothes," Darci said.

In the fall of our eighth-grade year, we hatched a plan to wear those clothes together to school. One of our moms took us on a shopping trip to Conway, and we came back with long, flowing skirts and dresses, floral pants, ruffled shirts, and chunky shoes from Payless. I got a big cross on a long velvet chain, and a choker necklace. I'd saved money from allowances and babysitting and diligently recorded when I'd accumulated enough to buy something, but a trip to Conway with that much cash was rare. With her working mom, Darci would get to shop at Maurice's, the trendy clothing store, but I couldn't afford things there unless I had money from Christmas.

As we walked down the school hallway in our trendy new gear, boys taunted us. I remember growing pink-faced with embarrassment.

"You'd think we just discovered America or something!" Darci

In late middle school, when Darci and I were thirteen and fourteen, we had a large group of friends, and she was at its center, being nice to everyone, avoiding most fights, and bringing people for sleepovers at her house. We all played junior high basketball, but because there was no gym at the middle school, we had to trudge up the hill to the high school, change, practice for thirty minutes, change back again with no shower because the gym had no functioning showers, eat lunch, and trudge back down. Adults turned us loose and trusted us to get where we were supposed to go. It was a long period of freedom and a respite from the drudgery of the day. We were always sleepy from our early school opening at seven-thirty a.m. On our walk back, our Southern school lunches of chicken and dumplings or Frito pie sat heavy in our bellies, and we were always drowsy and physically exhausted and a little silly. We passed Darci's house on the way, and it became familiar to all of us, almost as if it were part of the school itself.

As we walked along, chicken trucks barreled down the same road, noisy and too fast, leaving a trail of viscous, pinkish liquid. "Look at it, look at the goo!" Darci would yell, jumping nearly to the side of the road, giggling, sending us all into grossed-out hysterics. That's how everyone remembers her, boisterous and always in the middle. She would goof around. She'd walk with her knees together, eyes crossed, teeth bucked, hands forward, as if she were groping her way in the dark. "I can't see," she'd say with a heavy Southern yokel accent. This was hilarious to us. I knew she had learned her habit of performing from Ashley. Her life was shaped by her friendship with us, and ours by being friends with her.

I was always shyer than Darci. I thought I was fat and counted calories religiously in my journal, which made me self-conscious. The way we kept our diaries was indicative of our differing personalities. Darci, who was social and bubbly, kept a record of who she saw when, whereas I was more introspective and talked more about my feelings. Darci helped me with my shyness by bringing me along. In pictures of us together, she's always next to me, an arm around my shoulder, a reassuring hand on my knee. One year I was randomly assigned 104, the call numbers of our pop radio station, as a locker number. "That's so cool!" Darci said, pointing at my number. "You should get a K-Kick sticker!" She told every-body, "Monica has the coolest locker," to put me at ease.

Whenever Darci finished a sentence, she'd laugh and smirk and shrug, making it seem she didn't take anything too seriously. It had a way of putting people at ease. When someone messed her up in basketball practice, or if she was assigned a harder task on a group project in school, she never minded. "Thanks for that, friend," she'd say sarcastically, then laugh. She was always game. She was genuinely loyal, and people could usually count on her not to be mean. She would say, "Awww, Jayme's so sweet," and "Awww, I'm sorry you're sick," to soothe hurt feelings and bad days. She acknowledged effort and showed kindness in little ways that made people feel good around her. At least, that's how I remember her.

Darci and I went through the regular teenage agony that most girls experience at that age, but in our case it was influenced by our hometown's religious judgments and expectations. Impercep-tible to me at the time, a small crack appeared in our friendship then, one that would grow and lead to completely different lives for us as adults.

As an adult, it became my project to retrace our lives, Darci's and mine, to look for the fault lines that led from there to here, for what shaped our choices. At what point, if any, did I bear respon-sibility for what happened to Darci? Did I share any of the blame for the worst that befell her? What do I or any of us owe to the people we leave behind? For the well-being of my own soul, I needed to know: Did I have anything to atone for, and if so, what and how much?

4.

Boy Crazy

"Boy crazy" was what people called it. "She was so boy crazy." I never heard the reverse, that a boy was "girl crazy." Roughly half my middle and high school friends were "boy crazy," and it was changing their lives in dramatic and terrible ways.

Darci was one of the first to go boy crazy. When we were in sixth grade, one of her slightly older friends, who was fourteen, had a surprise baby. She'd been feeling sick, and her mom took her to the doctor, who said she was pregnant and due in a month. A few days after that, the girl went into labor in the bathroom, and she was rushed to the hospital. Her parents, longtime friends of Darci's parents, relayed this story in Darci's living room as the shocked and befuddled grandparents of a little boy just a few days old. I happened to be there and had an odd sense that this kind of family story was regular and normal in Clinton but also a vague awareness that it should not be so.

Darci was sad about the baby. She lamented in her diary that she rarely got to spend time with her friend anymore because the friend always had her baby and her boyfriend in tow. They were constantly kissing, she complained. "I guess I'll have to face it that things will never be the same again," she wrote. "I just wish I could go back and relive all the memories." She was young to have such a grown-up realization.

Girls regularly became pregnant in our middle and high schools, at least one a year. We always knew them because we knew everyone. They dropped out of school or graduated as mothers and sometimes as wives, bearing different names on their diplomas. Arkansas has had, and continues to have, one of the highest rates of teen pregnancy in the United States, even as the nationwide rate has declined since 1991.* The characteristics predictive of teen births tend to be the same regardless of race or ethnicity: teen mothers tend to live in communities where their mothers were young mothers themselves and to have only a high school degree. The neighborhoods are poorer, and employment levels are low. Wherever poverty exists, girls carry the burden of early motherhood.

In response to the high rate of teen births, the people of my hometown turned to the evangelical churches. In 1993 the Southern Baptists founded True Love Waits, an organization that promoted abstinence until marriage in place of comprehensive sex education. My friends began to wear "promise rings" in middle school, public signs of their pledge to remain virgins until they were married. Because some of them already had serious boyfriends, they dedicated these "promise rings" to their boyfriends, sort of as pre-engagement rings. In other words, we were thinking about marriage at thirteen and fourteen—before we were thinking about high school.

"For those who worked to sustain the old sexual order and re-

---

* In 2019, the most recent year available at the time I was writing this book, CDC numbers showed that Arkansas had the highest number of teen moms per capita, but in most years it competes for this distinction with its neighboring states—Mississippi, Louisiana, Oklahoma, Tennessee, Texas—and rates are also high in Appalachia, to Kentucky and West Virginia. In general, the rates of teen pregnancy are highest for Black and Latina girls, but because there are more white girls in the population, the numbers of young mothers in each group are nearly the same.

sisted models for sexual relationships and behaviors outside traditional marriage, a driving force has been fear," writes Marie Griffith in *Moral Combat*. "In the warfare over sex, the fear is typically one of three kinds: fear of increasing women's freedom, especially over their own bodies . . . white Protestant fear of encroaching religious or ethnic 'others,' . . . and a widespread and easily stoked fear that America is a once great nation now pitched into grave decline, largely because of the evil activities (very often, evil *sexual* activities) of some of its own citizens." It wasn't the last time fears about sexual freedom expressed themselves politically. And tied up with ideologies of xenophobia, nativism, and white supremacy, all those fears have had particular consequences for white Southern women. White nationalism and anti-abortion politics often go hand in hand. Rules and norms are created around white women, ostensibly to protect them, but they have, in truth, kept them down; at the same time, white women, near but not at the center of power, have throughout history helped enforce the very systems that subjugate them to the men in their communities. In Clinton, sex, and the question of whether we were allowed to have it or talk about it, was related to how people viewed girls' futures: Would we become fully realized adults, experiencing sexual freedom and fulfillment, or would we become helpmeets for our future husbands?

Outside the churches, the information we got was mostly misinformation. One day in seventh-grade health class, our teacher, who was also a football coach, drew a big circle on the board, and a tiny dot within it. "This circle is the microscopic holes in a condom," he said. "They're microscopic, and that means they're tiny. But guess what's even tinier?" he asked, pointing his chalk at the white dot on the green board. "AIDS. That's the AIDS virus, and it can get through those holes, and it will kill you. So the only way to not get AIDS is to not have sex." The message at church was that we had to keep ourselves pure for our husbands, and the message at school was that sex would either kill us or leave us pregnant, and there was nothing we could do to prevent either scenario except abstain. Even if girls having sex ended up neither pregnant nor dead, they would suffer damage to their reputation that would be hard to recover from.

Despite the sermons, my friends were still having sex at about the same rates as teenagers elsewhere in the country: just under half of teenagers report that they are sexually active before their eighteenth birthdays, according to the CDC. In Arkansas, they were having sex younger, though, and often without protection. Multiple studies have shown that abstinence-only education doesn't make teens less sexually active—and may actually make them more so at younger ages. It doesn't reduce the spread of sexually transmitted infections but may increase it. A 2017 study in the *Journal of Adolescent Health* concluded that promoting abstinence-only sex education is medically unethical and harms young people because it does not give them the tools to properly navigate their budding sexuality, or to prevent sexually transmitted infections or pregnancy.

Girls who did have sex were keenly aware that it was frowned on, and if a crisis resulted, they hesitated to seek help from an adult. In some cases, it kept them from breaking up with boyfriends. As if they were living in the Victorian era, they assumed that because they'd gone all the way with someone, they had to marry him. In seventh grade, when we were twelve and thirteen, one of our friends had a pregnancy scare. At the time, she was dating a boy from Shirley who was at least sixteen. She spent a day sick and upset in the girls' bathroom in sweatpants, worried that she might be pregnant. Her stomach was bothering her, and she was uncomfortable. She turned out not to be. But none of us thought to tell an adult, even though I knew of some who would have helped. We just worried for her and were relieved on her be-half when her fear passed. We were not even quite teenagers yet but were already navigating the full consequences of adult behav-ior alone.

I didn't know anything then about national trends, but I wit-nessed the consequences that studies could never quite capture: the fear of a fourteen-year-old girl stuck in a bathroom at school. We were vulnerable to exploitation and assault at early ages. I wouldn't have used those words then—I would have thought of these situations as the natural result of going boy crazy. The par-ticular boys we were dating, and kissing, and having sex with, al-most didn't matter, because they were in endless supply, and few of them ever faced any consequences. I tracked some of them down later and found that most did not remember these events with the same clarity that I did: the incidents that seemed so criti-cal to me just blended into the background for the boys. They did not have to navigate the repercussions, and sex was just an easy part of teenage-hood that ended early, with young marriages.

The girls who got pregnant were stigmatized—until their ba-bies were born. Then they were perceived as settled-down and adult and were revered as mothers. Our school was full of young moms who were still students, and those newly graduated would come back for ballgames and other events, babies on their hips. The girls still in school would pass their babies around, playing. It was an endless churn, baby after baby, born to the young and raised in families that spanned five or six generations because so few years separated grandmothers and mothers and daughters—and because the girls couldn't take care of them without help. All that mattered to people, it seemed, was the endless creation of life itself; the quality of it was never evaluated and never came into the equation.

I realized Darci was going boy crazy when we were twelve and she started sneaking out of her house at night. In her den—where we spent so many hours in easy companionship, played Twister, had sleepovers on the floor, watched forbidden scary movies and our MTV tapes—she took to hanging out with her older brother Cody and his friends. When they went to house parties on School Hill, she tagged along.

I sneaked out with Darci one night soon after my thirteenth birthday. I was sleeping over, but instead of going to sleep, we went into the bathroom and put on makeup. I used mocha-colored lipstick, the first my mom had let me buy, while Darci had an orange-tinted lipstick that set off her tanning-booth tan. She dotted foundation around her face, which had a bunch of moles—these were still the peak Cindy Crawford years, so beauty marks were glamorous. She fixed her hair so that it was wavy, gelled it to tame it, then tied it in a knot on top of her head. I put on a denim shirt and jeans.

Most likely Virginia and Darci's dad, Dennis, didn't hear us, as the den was far from their room. I was nervous and excited, all the more so once we got outside and felt the cool autumn night air. When you're a kid, something about being outside late at night when everyone else is asleep feels slightly dangerous—the familiar landscape cast in mysterious shadows but still easy to navigate. Darci played it casual, an old hand.

First we picked up a friend of her brother's whose parents were away, and who had the house to himself. He was in his bedroom getting ready to leave, and I kept giggling.

"Monica, you're like, 'Oh my God, I'm in a boy's house,'" she said, laughing.

"Shut up!" I was always nervous about boys and breaking rules. I knew I was hitching a ride on Darci's coolness: I was less popular than she was, and the older kids tolerated me only because of my proximity to her. She didn't mind it then. But sneaking out with her at night, though thrilling, also felt like courting danger, and I spent most of the evening uncomfortable, trying to decide how I felt about it all.

The three of us crossed the high school campus and the football field to a party house, a ramshackle old A-frame well past its tear-down date. Half a dozen kids were already there, mostly high school boys, drinking. More boys drifted in and out of the house, grabbing bottles of beer. It was my first party where people drank and smoked openly. I was nervous and bored. Darci said hi to everyone, made them laugh effortlessly, her charm sucking them in. Always shrugging and laughing at anything rude or bad, she never seemed to care deeply about anything and was always looking forward to the next fun she'd have. That was Darci's power, and it was enough for older kids and even some adults to find her good company. She was always at the center of the action. I realized that if she left me, she'd still have her own friends, while without her, I wouldn't know what to do.

But Darci's energy made her corruptible, and I can see, looking back, that she was a vulnerable child. She was only eleven the first time an older boy, who was fourteen, propositioned her for sex. She told him no, but the rest of her diary was a list of which boy she had a crush on, which boy she was sneaking out to ride around with, and which boy was obsessed with her. Sometimes she referred to them as stalkers, and she thought one of them broke a window in her house trying to get her attention one night. They were all much older than she was. When she was still twelve, she dated a sixteen-year-old whose father found out her age and made his son break up with her.

Another time she sneaked out to meet a boy she had a crush on at a party at a friend's house. Her crush was drunk. "It was actually kind of funny, but it didn't seem so funny when he started getting on top of me," she wrote in her diary. "But on the other hand he was so drunk that he wasn't strong enough to stay there." Later, the same boy would see her riding around with another older boy and chase her in his car. He followed her to the house where she was spending the night, banged on the door, and tried to force her out of the house by grabbing her wrist through a small opening and trying to pull her through. The casual violence of it shocked me when I read it as an adult. Yet Darci still thought about inviting him to her first formal dance.

At the party that night on School Hill, I saw a glimmer of this life when Darci abandoned me on the porch and sneaked away with one of the guys for a bit.

"Darci's cute," a high school sophomore named Josh said after she left.

"Come on," another said. "You have to wait till they have hair on their pussy."

I was mortified and ashamed and felt strongly that I had to get Darci away from here.

Finally she came back, and we went home. Back in the den, I told her that her new friends were sleazy. "That's not very nice, and not very Christian" was her response. "I thought we were trying to see the good in people."

Parties like that one were inevitably uncomfortable for me, largely because of my dad. I had realized he had a drinking problem when I was as young as four or five, while we still lived in the trailer in Shirley. He was working for a small company then, not making much money, and Momma had just had Courtney and quit work. It was a hard, strained time, with little money. Momma was often frustrated and, I realize now, lonely.

Daddy wasn't always home in time for dinner, so dinnertime was, like the long day that stretched before it, mostly girl time. I don't remember having a dining table—we ate off a low coffee table, parked between our couch and the TV. But on one of the rare nights Daddy joined us, he was talking funny and acting weird, and Momma was mad, in a different way than usual, and sad. Daddy was angry that supper was spaghetti and yelled.

"Daddy, what's wrong with you?" I asked, yelling too.

"You want to know what's wrong with me, Monica?" he yelled back.

Momma was in the kitchen and I could hear her quietly crying. Ashley and I were sobbing too.

"I'm drunk, that's what's wrong!" He got up and smashed his plate down, shattering it, and stomped off. He was wearing only a saggy pair of underwear, as he normally did when he was home, so he had to put his oil-stained work T-shirt and jeans back on before he opened the metal door and let it clang shut behind him.

White shards of the shattered plate, so thin they were almost translucent, were mixed into the red Prego sauce and spaghetti strands on the coffee table. Ashley and I cried over them. When I was little, I thought that when people were drunk they were drunk forever. Later, I learned that this is not true. Even later, I learned that sometimes it is.

After that night, Momma prohibited Daddy from drinking in the house, so some nights he didn't come home until late or even at all. When we kids were performing plays, or reading books, or going on explorations, or inventing new characters, he was with us maybe a quarter of the time.

More often he was in the corrugated-steel-framed garage that we called "the shop," with POTTS PLUMBING spray-painted in black on the outside. The shop was in the backyard that adjoined his mother's and stepfather's two small houses on School Hill. (They were divorced and lived apart.) Daddy used it as headquarters for his company but also as a place to sit and drink with his male relatives. Other times he made his way to the Mountain, where most of his extended family still lived. It was wooded and remote, near the old ghost town where his family was buried. No one bothered them at bonfires there, where they drank too much.

I was used to my dad not being at home—I thought most fathers weren't and that most of them drank too much. My mom judged his behavior harshly and blamed his family, but then so did others. Thanks to the teetotaler Baptists, Van Buren County had stayed dry even after Prohibition ended everywhere else; to buy liquor, wine, or beer, you had to drive twenty minutes to a county-line liquor store. In 2019, when a small group of residents began advocating for change, someone said of the group's chair, "I heard he's an alcoholic that don't want to drive to the Ridge."

When it came to liquor, there were two modes in Clinton: alcoholism or abstinence. This paralleled the bifurcated morality I saw everywhere: girls were either virgins or whores, students were either geniuses or failures, you could go to church or you could be a sinner. The town seemed to operate on two modes—the buttoned-up propriety of the churchgoers, who held power in the county, versus the rowdy hillbilliness of families like my dad's. What felt like a rigid divide allowed no room for missteps, or subtleties, or in-betweenness.

Seen from a distance, everyone in Van Buren County looks poor or working class. The average family lives near poverty or only slightly above it, and an unexpected event can destabilize its situation quickly. The poverty rate has stayed at just under 20 percent since the 1970s, and the median household income in 2019 was just over $38,000, which is within 200 percent of the federal poverty line for a family of four. Ranked by income, Van Buren is in the bottom half of the state's counties, a poor county in a poor state. But for families with a tenuous grasp on the middle class, financial stability seems just within reach. It is a poor place, but not wholly impoverished.

People in Clinton tended to blame poverty on perceived moral failings, but they tolerated behavior in children of the wealthy that they didn't tolerate in the poor. In our small town, unlike a big suburb, we were all together, walking the same school hallways, in a stepped-down microcosm of America's class system. Everyone's place was transparent to everyone else on a daily basis. Clinton was self-contained, and everyone knew everything about everyone else, or seemed to: who you dated, where you bought your clothes, how you acted on weekends. It seemed at times they also knew your destiny.

Children and teenagers were sorted into another binary as well: the upstanding citizens and the ne'er-do-wells. The "good" kids were those bound for college. They avoided partying or did it only discreetly, played sports, spent nights and weekends at ballgames and church events, and formed monogamous relationships early. Parents encouraged their teenage relationships, chaperoning and ushering them on dates and folding them into family events. Their families went to church every Sunday, nicely dressed in church clothes, and went to lunch afterward at the Ozark Café or some other restaurant in town, or to a grandmother's house for a pot roast. Those students were destined to enter adult life early, marry at a young age, and move seamlessly into roles their parents fulfilled: teachers, doctors, dentists. Their social spots seemed almost inherited.

My friend April, who moved back to Clinton to raise her two children, saw this clearly as an adult. "Like, Kid A: 'We're thinking you'll go to college and make something out of yourself, so we'll put more effort into you.'" Her own kids benefited from the reputation she'd had as a good student. The teachers, who were her peers and sometimes friends from her own school days, automatically trusted her.

By contrast, the "bad" kids were those who sneaked out of their homes and partied on weekends. It was an unspoken assumption that they wouldn't make it to college. They got into trouble at school. We kids gossiped about them, and so did some of the adults. As April put it, "Kid B: 'Well, you come from a line of poverty and living off the system, so we'll just hope you don't get knocked up.'" It could be hard, living in a small town like ours, to escape family history. "I don't think it's spoken," April said, "but it's kind of hard not to pass that history on in a lot of ways."

She told me that two boys from her class—rowdy, athletic, good-natured class clowns and troublemakers—now had young sons of their own in the same class at school. A teacher looked at the young pair and joked, "Here we go again!" Everyone laughed, as if the sons would inevitably be the same as the fathers—the same story would play over and over with each new generation. Seeing this cycle helped me understand why my mom had felt strongly about cutting off my dad's family, and why I had been so careful not to follow in what I thought were his footsteps. People who tried to break the pattern were often alone, set against the larger forces of small-town thinking and small-town gossip.

Darci was getting a reputation as a partier, and hanging out with her became increasingly fraught. During Darci's fourteenth birthday slumber party, half the girls sneaked out and half didn't. After that, the "good" girls stopped going to Darci's house. They also avoided Thriftway parking lot parties, where teenagers sat in cars and got drunk and hooked up. Instead, the "good" kids had serious boyfriends and wore promise rings. Their lives were already revolving around their futures as wives and mothers, regardless of any potential career.

As a child, I felt trapped by this system. I didn't want to be judged by those around me, but I didn't have the power to ignore their judgments, so I became judgmental too. And though I never really fit in with either the "good" kids or the partiers, I decided to align with the "good" kids. Today it's sometimes painful, or laughable, to look back at how severe I was. I didn't believe in the religious prohibitions on sex before marriage, but I did see the social consequences in Clinton that those who failed to follow them suffered. I can see now that I had few options as a teenager. I was still close to Darci, but in order to make sure others saw the differences between us, I was more judgmental than I might have been. I also felt that in a town where people married and had children young, teenagers' missteps carried a lot of weight.

My mom started to set boundaries around us too. When I was fourteen and Ashley was thirteen, Darci asked us to go with her to a concert in Little Rock that some older high school girls had invited her to. The teenagers were going to drive us all. Momma said we couldn't go.

Virginia challenged my mom, saying she'd feel more comfortable letting Darci go if we went too.

"Well, you'll just have to tell her no, too, then," Momma said.

Virginia got emotional and said she couldn't tell Darci no because it was too difficult. "You don't understand how she screams at me," she said, according to my mom. In more dire situations, Virginia would throw her hands up and say, "I can't make her do something she doesn't want to do."

This was what I remember most about Virginia from that time. Darci's parents normally left us alone, even when we were in her den. But when Darci wanted something from Virginia, and Virginia refused, she screamed at her mother and disrespected her in ways that seemed over the top even to us. Virginia was unable to stand up to her. As teenage girls, most of us also fought with our moms, but if we'd ever acted like Darci did, a torrent of punishments, spankings, and groundings would have been visited upon us.

• • •

I sneaked out with Darci only once or twice, finding it troubling and not fun. We reached an unspoken agreement that I didn't want to know about her partying because I didn't approve, but I also didn't want to tattle. This left me in the dark about how risky her worst behavior became. Our friend Vanessa Allen, who was maybe the most boy crazy of us all, snuck out with Darci. In my journal, I wondered, "Which of our friends will get pregnant first? My money is on Erica or Vanessa."

Vanessa had long, curly black hair and brown eyes and was the oldest of four kids. Her mom, Susie, had gotten married as a teenager and had Vanessa when she was eighteen. When I spoke to Susie in the summer of 2017, she told me that when her kids were young, she struggled to pay the bills. But by the time I knew Vanessa, Susie had already gone to cosmetology school and worked as a hairdresser. In my memory, Susie is always bouncing around a stylist's chair, in a constant, bubbly flow of conversation and gossip, her own hair poodle-curly, half pulled up in a barrette, with a perpetual tan from the salon's tanning bed, which she charged clients to use.

Vanessa's family belonged to the evangelical Church of Christ. When we were older, her dad, who used to bag groceries at the Piggly Wiggly, became a minister there. Vanessa wore a promise ring in middle school, vowing not to have sex before marriage. But she liked attention from boys. She always had boyfriends and had a reputation for being a flirt. I remember her wearing a tight-fitting bodysuit at a football game. When she walked past a group of grown men, they whistled at her, and one of them said admiringly, "Someone's been eating her beans and cornbread!" She was fourteen. Vanessa turned pink with embarrassed pride and shame that she didn't know quite what to do with.

Throughout our childhoods, adults had taught us girls to keep boys from touching us before marriage, but no one ever told us what to do if we wanted to touch them. No one acknowledged our own desires, and Vanessa, more than any of us, had to navigate that space on her own, trying to determine what she wanted and what she didn't.

The first time Vanessa had sex, it was at her house while her parents were still at work: she'd asked her boyfriend to stop, and he hadn't. Later, with other boys, Vanessa sometimes felt like she couldn't say no to their advances because she'd already lost her virginity, although she'd only gone all the way with one other boyfriend. Only many years later did Vanessa recognize some of these incidents as sexual assaults. She didn't blame the boys necessarily; they were just doing what everyone expected them to do, she felt. But her reputation suffered. The hard part for her was that she didn't hate sexual experimentation; she just didn't think she should be enjoying it so much. In that space, between her desire and her shame, other girls smelled blood.

At Christmastime one year, she wore a Santa shirt that said HO HO HO across the front, and one of our friends pointed to it and said, "Hey, that's right! Ho ho ho," and everyone laughed. Vanessa went to the office, sobbing, and called her mom for a new shirt.

This slight expression of social disapproval pushed Vanessa and Darci closer. One night when we were twelve or thirteen, Vanessa was having a sleepover at Darci's house when Susie got a call in the middle of the night. "Do you know where your daughter is?" a voice asked, and then the caller hung up.

Susie went into town and knocked on car doors in places where teenagers hung out: "Hello, have you seen my daughter?!?" She found Vanessa in the Exxon station parking lot, in a red truck with a twenty-four-year-old guy. She did not know exactly what they were doing, but she pulled Vanessa out. Susie remembers grabbing her arm, but Vanessa remembers that her mother pulled her by the hair, slapped her face, and took her home.

Vanessa was grounded for a year and faced other consequences too: Vanessa going boy crazy was a problem that Susie decided to solve. Once Vanessa came to school exhausted because Susie had driven her to Little Rock the night before and parked outside a home for troubled teens we'd seen advertised on TV, threatening to leave her there.

Darci, on the other hand, rarely got caught and rarely faced consequences when she did. Her den became a twenty-four-hour teenage clubhouse, complete with alcohol and, later, drugs. We all knew Virginia and Dennis were willfully blind to it, but we didn't know why.

When I spoke to Susie as an adult, she still agonized over those years. Had she been too hard on Vanessa, or not hard enough, or hard in the wrong ways? She blamed herself for the worst that happened to her daughter in the years that followed, but she also knew that, transported back in time, she'd probably make the same choices again. She'd tried to do what she thought was in her daughter's best interest.

Susie's remorse over Vanessa contrasted with Virginia's thoughts about Darci's childhood. Soon after I reconnected with Darci, I reached out to Virginia. We talked about how Darci was doing, which at the time was not well. "It seems like everyone wants to blame the mother for their kids' problems," Virginia said, then asked, "Are you going to blame me for what happened to Darci?" I told her I agreed that people were often too quick to blame moms, and it was unfair. But later my feelings would grow more complicated, as I observed more of the dynamic between her and Darci. "Darci made her own choices," Virginia insisted.

Virginia and I stayed in frequent contact in the years following, and whenever we spoke about Darci, she referred to her daughter's "decisions" and "choices." It troubled me that she so casu-ally referred to Darci's teenage behavior as "choices." Most parents would have limited their daughters' options, given that they were still children, still learning and growing. It took me a few more years to understand why Virginia dismissed any qualms about her own role as Darci's mom, and how that had shaped my friend.

• • •

In 1994, the summer after we finished middle school, Darci broke my heart. In those months, she and I and our friends often went to Greers Ferry Lake, and if we were lucky and had a friend whose parents had access to a boat, we'd go out for a day of waterskiing. Otherwise Virginia would drive us to the swimming area, set up a lawn chair on the makeshift beach, and read whatever mystery she'd gotten from the library. We'd make our way out to the buoy that marked off the swimming area, a long orange floating tube. We'd sit on it or hang off it while chatting out of Virginia's ear-shot. There was no lifeguard, and I couldn't really swim well. If my mom had been there, she wouldn't have let me dog-paddle out with my friends. Without her, though, I felt very adult and free.

One day late in the summer, Darci and I and some friends were in the lake's swimming area. The oppressive August heat seemed to keep us from moving fast or taking full breaths. The water was barely an escape; the swimming area, a vast expanse of green water, was warm. We walked a good distance out, kicking up slimy mud from the bottom, negotiating the minnows that nib-bled at our feet, then made our way to the buoy.

The lake fills an area of the valley formerly known as the Big Bottoms, which had once comprised five fertile farming commu-nities. Darci and I had read in Mr. Duncan's *History of Van Buren*

County that when the Army Corps of Engineers built the lake, it hadn't exhumed the bodies from the communities' cemeteries but just let the lake fill in above them. On that day, as on most days, we plunged as far down as we could and opened our eyes, terrifying ourselves with thoughts of what we might see.

That day we sat in a line, single file, on the buoy, chatting mostly with the person next to us. I was sitting next to our friend Erica when she casually dropped the news that Darci had lost her virginity. Darci, she said, had been hanging out with Robbie, one of Cody's eighteen-year-old friends, in her den. One night they had started kissing, and one thing led to another. Darci was only fourteen.

My heart was pounding, and I must have looked shocked.

"Didn't you know?" Erica asked. But she could see on my face that I didn't.

I felt betrayed, both because it had happened and because Darci hadn't told me. Did she not trust me anymore? We'd always talked about boys, and who we were flirting with, and who we had crushes on; I had no idea who this Robbie even was.

After a while I moved farther down the buoy to where Darci was sitting and chatted with her nonchalantly. The other girls, forming their own little group, floated off and left us alone.

"Darci," I said, trying to contain my anger and hurt. "Why Robbie?"

"It's no big deal." She shrugged and laughed. "I didn't think you would approve. He's kind of gangsta."

Robbie was one of a group of five or six boys, all unrelated, who'd moved to Clinton from California in the past few years. Our principal, Mr. Hutto, was convinced they belonged to gangs and were bringing gang activity with them, because they sagged their pants and wore their hats backward. He made us watch informational videos on how not to succumb to peer pressure to join a gang. "These boys, I don't know what kind of culture they're bringing here," Mr. Hutto used to fret. We made endless fun of him. The hysteria over gangs in my small town was the first of many such episodes—over Satanism, child trafficking—things unrelated to the actual dangers that teenagers in town faced.

"I always thought you'd disapprove," Darci continued, "like I was one of your little sisters."

I did disapprove, but mostly I was concerned for her. It felt like she was abandoning her dream of going to California, in order to hang out with a boy from California. It felt like her life was being consumed by unimportant things. Boys. Sex. Drinking. Partying. In what kind of life could she do those things and not get stuck in town? The girls who had babies and got married never left Clinton. My mom had always warned me about those traps, and she didn't seem wrong. Where was the Darci I'd known who couldn't wait to get out of Clinton? Why didn't she understand that leaving our hometown would demand the entire force of our beings, that she couldn't waste energy on things that didn't propel her outward? And most important to me at the time, where would her new friends and new boyfriend and new way of life leave me?

Darci had crossed an invisible line, I felt. Girls were expected to act a certain way, and as she continued to "make bad choices," as people would say, fewer and fewer of our friends' moms would let them hang out with her. Finally Darci would find herself among people who didn't care, who partied even more than she did. I thought about this a lot in later years, as people my age who raised teenagers in Clinton told me about who they wouldn't let their daughters hang out with, where they didn't allow them to go. The girls who found themselves on the wrong side of that line faced a lot of judgment and had a harder time.

I made myself smile as I watched Darci plunge into the water, feet first, straight as a dart. But inside I was devastated and knew I couldn't easily fix what had broken.

• • •

Vanessa was the first in our group to suffer the public consequences of going boy crazy. Her mom, Susie, later told me that older boys took advantage of her. "I know she was very flirty," she remembered. "I don't know how many relationships she had. But . . . she was definitely targeted. Maybe because she was cute, big-breasted, or flirty, I don't know. It was stressful." Boys would come by the house looking for Vanessa, and Susie would yell at them, "She's not a dog in heat!" She remembers trying to talk to their parents, who just blamed Vanessa.

The following summer, just after our ninth-grade year, fifteen-year-old Vanessa and her parents went to Colorado to visit family. At the church, they met the preacher's son who Vanessa and Susie thought was about nineteen. He and Vanessa hit it off, and after she returned to Arkansas, they kept in touch. Later that fall, in 1995, near the end of the first semester of our sophomore year, he traveled to Arkansas and stopped to visit. He asked Vanessa to marry him, and she said yes. She found out then that he was twenty-four—but he was a good Christian, she thought, so the age difference didn't matter. Vanessa liked him, and she was ready to leave Clinton. She knew that people in town speculated about her love life and called her a whore, and that if she stayed in town and kept having boyfriends, they'd continue to call her one. They wouldn't be able to do that if she moved to Colorado and became a wife.

Nevertheless, her engagement was a scandal. "Vanessa has lost her mind," Darci said when she told me the news, and we wanted to talk her out of it. A group of us on a bus to a basketball game tried to convince her to change her mind. "How do you know he's not an ax murderer?" Vanessa remembers me asking, though I remember Darci asking that.

"I know him!" she insisted.

But she'd only seen him twice, and he was too old, we insisted. She was too young. What about school?

Vanessa got up. "Let's go, Rena," she said to the only girl who stuck by her, and stormed to the front of the bus, away from us. "I know they want to talk about me behind my back, and that's okay."

At first, to be near her new fiancé Vanessa arranged to live with someone else in Colorado, but when that fell through, they decided to rush their marriage so they could live together. She came back home and picked a day for her wedding in January 1996 that conflicted with a basketball game, so few of her friends could go. "In seventeen days, Vanessa's life is over," I wrote in my journal. "One of my longest and oldest friends, and I am sitting back and watching her end it." Vanessa had to be married across the border in Missouri, because even Arkansas didn't allow girls to be married at fifteen, even with parental permission. Vanessa's parents not only gave their permission, but her dad, a minister, performed the ceremony.

In the pictures she showed us later, she looks impossibly young, arm in arm with a grown man we'd never met. "Vanessa's gone and I'll probably never see her again," I wrote in my journal. We were all gutted by the loss of her and her friendship, and also by the subtle message that we were all vulnerable. Susie had allowed it to happen because she believed Vanessa was boy crazy and veering toward disaster and because the boys she was hanging out with partied too much.

Years later, when I visited Susie in her salon, she said allowing

Vanessa to marry was the biggest regret of her life. "I guess the biggest thing about regrets is, you gotta go back to that time and think about why you made that decision," she said, crying. It had seemed obvious to me, even as a teenager, that a grown man who wanted to marry a fifteen-year-old was suspect at best. But for Susie, the fact that Vanessa's husband had come from a Christian family they'd known for a long time, a family who had worked as missionaries, was enough. And it had been imperative to get her out of Clinton. Three kids had been killed in Clinton that year, Susie remembered. Some of them died drinking and driving. Usually boys did the drinking and driving, but they had girls like Darci and Vanessa in their trucks with them.

"I just had a gut feeling that if I kept her home, if I did not let her go, she would end up dead," Susie told me. "Can any parent stop a fifteen-year-old, or sixteen-year-old, from doing what they want to do?"

Vanessa's hasty marriage came early in our high school years, just as the rest of us were trying to figure out our relationships to our own dreams. But it wasn't unheard of in town for a fifteen-year-old to marry. Over the next few years, more of my friends would become wives, many before they turned eighteen. For me, high school was a launchpad for going to college and having a career. For other girls, it was just a four-year holding pattern until real life started, a life focused on marriage and children. Middle school would be the last time we'd worry about whose parents would drive us to the lake. Over the next few years, we would have to make adult decisions with adult consequences.

5.

The Rebellion

Early in high school, Darci and I continued to be star students together, both of us making straight A's. Darci was a natural leader and often led the basketball team and other groups we found ourselves in. We took dance lessons together and traveled to perform as cloggers in talent shows and competitions. Dance school doubled as a place where future pageant girls learned their skills and where we all learned to wear makeup. Our dance teacher used to say, half-jokingly, "Girls, I'm here to tell you, you can marry more money in a day than you can make in a lifetime," though both her daughters would grow up to have successful careers in broadcasting. Later, we'd perform as cloggers at folk festivals and at county and state fairs, as well as the Grand Ole Opry, Disneyland, and the Macy's Thanksgiving Day Parade. Darci wanted to succeed in dance. "Everybody told me I did good, but I don't think I was really that good," she wrote in her diary after her first recital. "I think I could do better." I remember her having a try-hard attitude like that in her younger years, when she wanted to excel.

During the first two years of high school, Darci and I were still close, at least within certain parameters. Aside from dance, we took many of the same classes. We sat together at lunch, in a school cafeteria, probably like all school cafeterias, that was organized by cliques. On one side were the preppy kids who did well in school and always played sports or were on the cheerleading squad. On the other were the rednecks who wore cowboy boots and took agriculture classes and joined Future Farmers of America. These factions more or less aligned with family socioeconomic levels. There was also a group of artistic kids, many of whom played in the school band, and they sometimes overlapped with the other two groups. Our school's small size limited our social groups, sometimes making it hard for someone to find a place to fit in, especially because so much of town life revolved around organized sports. It made it hard for me.

From our table near the back of the cafeteria, Darci and I would watch the long row of older boys, cowboys, eating lunch. Darci gave them all internal monologues. *Mmmmm, Momma's home cooking,* one of them, the son of the cafeteria cook, would say to himself. One of the boys on the Mountain got an internal life that indicated an encyclopedic knowledge of farm animals: *Well now, what you see here is a heifer that . . .* and we'd make up a long, involved story about his poor imagined cow. It was silly and fun and a little mean, in the way teenage girls can be.

Darci had always been funny. When we had psychology class together, during a lesson on Freud, we learned that he thought nearly every action was the result of an unconscious, suppressed sexual desire. "So what?" Darci blurted out in class. "You murder someone and then you just say, 'It's okay, I'm a pervert' and get out of trouble?" Everyone laughed.

On the surface at least, Darci remained committed to getting out of Clinton. When a friend told us she was going to leave school and move to New York or Los Angeles to be an actress, Darci said, tenderly but bluntly, "That's the worst plan I've ever heard."

I reminded her, "Just a few months ago you were talking about joining the navy so that they could pay for your college!"

The girl started crying and said she really just wanted to get away from her parents. Darci and I tried to convince her that staying in school was the only way to have a different life than theirs.

"I guess I'm lucky because I don't know what it's like to want to get away from your parents," I said to Darci later.

She and I agreed on some issues in ways that put us at odds with the community as a whole. Once in a class, Darci told me, a conversation had drifted to the topic of abortion. A classmate said that if she ever had a daughter and found out she was having sex as a teenager, she would rather kill her than let her have an abortion. "That's a real Christian attitude," Darci quipped. Darci and I were unusual in this regard, liberal for the town, less concerned with enforcing a moral code.

Early in my sophomore year, I took the ACT for practice, and I talked Darci into taking it too. The day she got her scores, she came to tell me. I was in Spanish class, and she knocked on the window. I got up to see her briefly, annoying the teacher.

"I got a twenty-two!" she told me when I opened the door. A 22 is an above-average score on the ACT, which maxes out at 36 and is graded on a bell curve, like the SAT. It's a high score for a sophomore.

I felt as though the ACT would unlock opportunities for me, and I hoped Darci would grab on to her success and see the possibilities in it too. I gave her a hug. "I knew you could do it!" I said. "I'm so proud of you."

Later we told our dance teacher. "Yeah," she said, satisfied. "My girls are smart."

Darci started to look up colleges in California, and, for some reason that she didn't share, she settled on Claremont McKenna, a small liberal arts college in southern California. She'd found it the way we used to find towns in our atlas and was drawn to it the way we'd once been drawn to those faraway boldfaced names on the map. She wanted me to apply there; I wanted her to. "It feels like something's waiting for me there," she said. "I don't know what." I remember the force of my hope for her, willing her to hold on to her dream and apply to college somewhere in California. I thought if I stayed close to her, if we talked about our dreams enough, it would work out. Maybe she could withstand the distractions of boys and partying and get herself to California.

What I wanted to do, more than anything, was find a way to help. "I've about determined that it's time to do something about Darci," I wrote in my journal during our sophomore year. "I feel like I'm the closest one to her now. The main problem I see is that she thinks I'm naive, and probably won't listen to me when it comes to something she thinks she knows more about." She was drinking and smoking by then. I designed a one-woman intervention to convince her to stop doing all the things I thought would keep her from going to college.

But after I wrote that in my journal, I didn't say anything to her. For the next couple of years, I would continue to worry about her, make up my mind to confront her, and then not do it. One day at lunch, I did screw up enough courage to talk to her, to tell her that I worried her future would be derailed by her drinking and partying, that I thought she could go to college in California if she wanted to and that she had to work for it. But at that moment two of her older friends came over and joined us at our table. So I got up and walked away, afraid to say anything before an audience.

Despite her good grades, Darci seemed to be struggling in ways I didn't entirely understand. Freshman year Erica and I argued with her about something, I don't remember what, but I wrote in my journal, "The other day, she was in a really bad mood, and her and Erica got kind of into a fight. . . . She started skitzing out, talking about how she couldn't please everybody and she couldn't take the pressure." But I didn't ask Darci what I wanted so very much to ask: What was going wrong?

The summer before our sophomore year, Darci called to tell me about a plan. I stood in the kitchen holding our wireless phone, the antenna pulled out, as my family buzzed around me. "I'm quitting basketball," she said. "It was just taking up far, far too much of my time for an extracurricular activity."

"But you love being on the team!" I said, genuinely shocked.

"I dread practice every day," she said. "I don't want to do something that will make me miserable."

I paused. I had felt the same way. My journal was full of lamentations about the anxiety basketball had caused me. I dreaded practice. Yet it had been hard to quit, because at our school we were expected to play a sport and have "school spirit." Suspicion fell on students who did not, so when I quit basketball, I was quick to take up something else—I joined the cheerleading squad.

"Those are all the reasons I quit too," I said. "But Darci, you're actually good at basketball."

"Maybe, but I don't love it," she said. "I think that, if something's going to demand that much of you, you should love it."

We hung up, and I told my mom. In her worrying, fretting way, she pursed her lips. "Well, she won't have any reason to go to school once she quits basketball."

"What? Her grades are wonderful!" I said. "She's so smart and has so much going for her."

Momma shrugged. "What if it's not enough to keep her there?"

Adults said this frequently: the fun offered by sports was a way to keep kids in school, sort of a bribe. These were the years before the No Child Left Behind legislation created incentives to keep students in school until graduation. In 1990 the high school graduation rate in Arkansas was just under 77 percent.* Students dropped out for many reasons, and at the time, they were usually allowed to just leave.

Once she quit basketball, Darci did start missing school on random days, especially in our junior and senior years. And if something was hard or frustrating, she'd just stop doing it, the way she'd quit basketball. Classes did become harder, and Darci was easily frustrated when she didn't pick something up right away, so she stopped taking the harder science and math classes and took fewer electives. She hung out with me and my family less often. She stopped dressing up for school and often looked like she'd barely rolled out of bed, throwing on jeans and whatever shirt she could find. She usually looked tired.

By the end of our sophomore year, Darci was speaking about college as if it were only optional. "I don't know how to study," she said during one lunch, shrugging her shoulders as if it didn't matter. *Darci's showing signs of giving up,* I thought. I wrote about it in my journal as a disappointment but also as if it didn't surprise me, as if Darci were following a pattern I'd seen in older students, who were ground down before high school ended. But I pushed down what I felt about seeing Darci go through this.

In more than twenty years of study, the education researchers David and Myra Sadker have shown the subtle and unsubtle ways schools discriminate against girls. When girls are quiet and follow the rules, their behavior often goes unremarked because girls are expected to act that way. Boys are more often disciplined for misbehavior, but when they are, they receive constructive criticism.

---

* High school graduation rates are often unreliable and vary from school to school—they typically count only people who began taking classes during their senior year, so they miss students who left school in earlier years.

Girls are subtly discouraged from taking risks, which inhibits their ability to learn. Over time they see in their schoolbooks that it's mainly the men who make history and record it. The American Association of University Women, in its landmark survey *How Schools Shortchange Girls,* originally published in 1992, when Darci and I were in middle school, found that girls' self-esteem takes a free fall after elementary school. Only 37 percent of girls told the Sadkers and their colleagues they were happy with themselves at this point, and only 29 percent said they felt this way in high school. Girls are pressured to be pretty and attractive, which starts to consume their attention at school. These issues are common to many schools across the country, but the stakes are higher for low-income communities, where family connections and family money will not make up for the areas where schools fail girls.

When girls don't act in the ways they're expected to or when they are perceived to be acting out, they're punished.* Any one individual teacher might not be sexist or racist, but the education system is: teachers belong to the same culture as everyone else, and it can shape the way they view behavior and achievement. School can become a place where society's problems are replicated. Teachers call on boys more often than girls, the Sadkers documented, and pay attention to their students in slightly different ways: they compliment girls on their clothing but boys on their achievements. Girls succeed or struggle in school according to the expectations society sets for them. Sometimes these attitudes are explicit, but more often they're humming quietly in the background, unnoticed. The hum grows louder and clearer over

---

* Black girls tend to be punished in school more often than their white counterparts and are frequently pushed out of school. Black boys, similarly, tend to be punished more often and more harshly than their white peers.

the years, until we find ourselves singing the same song, uncertain of how we learned it.

I watched these dynamics play out as my friend group started to fracture based on our social lives, as classes became more difficult and required more effort, and as we all started to believe we were bad at math. We absorbed the lesson that we weren't cut out for science. Our confidence in our ability to do anything—from athletics to academics—faltered. We didn't give up on school entirely, but we modified our goals and reined in our dreams.

In high school, one of our male science teachers frequently told us that the best career for women was to be a teacher because we'd get the same holidays as our kids. He was one of the few male teachers in the school. He also told us, as if it were scientific fact, that women had an extra layer of fat on their bodies, which was why they had an easier time tolerating hot dishwater. He always said it with a facetious grin, but it still made me angry. "Oh, he's just joking," people would say when I complained, so I'd drop it. But I couldn't entirely; it helped fuel my desire to leave behind not just Clinton but the worldview it espoused that so diminished women and their achievements.

As Darci pulled away from me, I grew incredibly lonely. "The only person I really feel like I can share my feelings with is Darci, and . . . I don't completely trust her anymore," I wrote in my journal. We'd both always talked about getting out of Clinton. But while I'd decided to leave by going to college far away, Darci found another way to leave: by ceasing to care, by rejecting everything about Clinton, even its rules and expectations for her.

Later, when I asked teachers what they remembered about Darci, their answer was always the same. Virginia seemed like a normal mom, and Darci seemed like she had it together. Darci was a smart girl, and that's how she was labeled. She did not seem to be suffering and seemed well cared for. She was handling her schoolwork. The school was full of students with dire problems: They didn't have food or electricity or running water at home. They never showed up. They seemed unable to read, even in high school. Their parents had serious mental health issues. They were pregnant. Under the circumstances, Darci flew under the radar.

It was Darci's ability to mask her emotional troubles, as a high school student, that kept people, even me, from intervening. That her problems were metastasizing became obvious only in retrospect. And my family had its own crisis emerging.

• • •

In elementary school, Ashley had outbursts and a wild energy that sometimes would not be contained. She got reprimanded for being loud, speaking out of turn, and causing problems at recess. At some point, my parents took her to doctors to see if she had attention-deficit/hyperactivity disorder, or ADHD. They always came back empty-handed, without a diagnosis or Ritalin, which was the ADHD treatment drug of choice in the 1990s.

When Ashley was in fifth or sixth grade, her body would convulse at regular intervals, in an elaborate series of movements and sounds that seemed like a controlled mini-seizure. She'd hunch up her shoulders, roll her head to the side and around, roll her eyes to the back of her head, and make squeaking sounds. Sometimes she'd lick her hands as a finishing touch. If you remarked on this strange ceremony, she'd always laugh and look apologetic, confused by her own actions. Her teachers called my parents in for a conference. They thought she had a brain tumor.

About three years into their search for a diagnosis, my parents took her to Arkansas Children's Hospital in Little Rock, which had a charity program, to be evaluated. Then on one of our Saturday walks around the empty high school campus, Darci came up with a diagnosis. She told me about an episode of *The Maury Povich Show* in which people were onstage, screaming out taboo words, like curse words and racist words, and jerking their bodies around like Ashley did. They said they couldn't control it. They had a disease called Tourette syndrome. "I think that's what Ashley has!" Darci said.

My first reaction was embarrassment, discomfort at the idea that Ashley had a problem that everyone could see.

But Darci was right—that was the very diagnosis Ashley received after months of tests and evaluations. Tourette syndrome is unusual, a hiccup in the brain's circuitry that looks like an impulse-control problem, and there weren't many treatments for it. Ashley's tics were involuntary. But because they often took the form of familiar sounds and words and what looked like controlled movements, it could seem like she was just misbehaving. Though Ashley had begun exhibiting symptoms around the time she started school, they'd peaked at age ten and eleven, which is typical of the disorder.

After Ashley's diagnosis, Momma brought experts to the school to meet with Ashley's teachers. She visited the classrooms and counselor's offices to get special dispensations for Ashley for tests, untimed and free of distractions. Her grades improved. School was still hard for her. In ninth grade, her math teacher gave her detention for "bawking like a chicken in class." Momma went over to the school, complained, and got her punishment lifted. Other students alternately teased and revered her. They enjoyed her outbursts when they thought she was funny, but they were less impressed when they weren't in the mood.

Momma would never have said that I was smart and Ashley wasn't. She saw the differences between us, to some extent, as differences in ability, but she was also clear about the way circumstances affected our performance in school. She never thought

Ashley's struggles were divinely determined, as many did; nor did she allow anyone, including us, to use Ashley's medical condition as an excuse to not help her excel. She made Ashley try harder on her schoolwork. She encouraged her to try new things and to explore her interests, which included drama and theater. She did that with all of us. For years Ashley took piano lessons from Darci's mom—Virginia taught a few students for extra cash after her workday ended—despite having no talent; I wasn't allowed to quit the marching band until ninth grade ended and I'd fulfilled my commitment to the junior high teams; every year after we turned three, we took dance classes, and somehow Momma and Daddy always found the money for us to join the dance school trips out of state. I can't think of a single time my mom said something just was or wasn't "the way things were"; she always set her sights on what could be. It was a constant struggle for my parents, both in money and time, and they had no particular reason to believe it would pay off.

As Ashley grew older, she was increasingly medicated, and her sleep became irregular. She was on antidepressants and experimental treatments, like nicotine patches. Sometimes she'd sleep for days, and sometimes not at all, especially after she started high school. On mornings when she couldn't wake up, probably in part because of the medication, Momma went in yelling and screaming and dragged her out of her room and down the stairs. Some mornings she put her clothes on for her. Ashley as a teenager had grown tall, five foot eight. Sometimes when Momma fought her, she would go limp like a noodle and let herself be dragged through the house. But every morning Momma got her to school and made sure that once she was there, she at least had a fair shot.

• • •

As my family fretted over Ashley's diagnosis and her progress in school, we became more insular, more focused on taking care of ourselves. Courtney went through her own middle school travails mostly unnoticed. In those years, while my parents' attention was on Ashley, mine was on leaving town.

Outside school, Darci just sort of dropped away from my orbit. She was dating Robin Lemmonds but kept that relationship from me as part of her effort to shield me from her new life. Robin had come to Arkansas from Omaha and was into skateboarding and smoking pot. He seemed cool, wore baggy pants, and had a bit of a troublemaker reputation.

In 2015 I got in touch with Robin, who told me he had hated Arkansas and was bored in the countryside: "You couldn't express yourself creatively at all because you were always labeled something very derogatory." He'd wanted to study art but found few opportunities in Clinton. He got called a "faggot" more times than he'd ever been called any name anywhere else. "You didn't have creative outlets like art and music. You couldn't even skateboard." He spent a lot of time in the nearby college city of Conway, where he was part of the skateboarding community.

In 1994 a documentary called *Bangin' in Little Rock* called attention to gangs in our state capital, which had a higher per capita violent crime rate than the national average. Both the movie and the elevated crime rate fed urban legends about "gang culture" in Little Rock: that you mustn't visit at night, or flash your car lights or you'd be killed in a gang initiation, and you must never park in the mall's underground parking garage.

Little Rock was, and still is, almost exactly half Black and half white, with only small populations of other groups. Today the city is still largely segregated by race and is a gateway to the majority Black counties of the Arkansas Delta, along the Mississippi. White people in rural areas like Clinton believed that Little

Rock, like all cities, was dangerous, and they called it names that included a racist epithet. They lived in fear that a corrupting urban influence would come into their small town.

So when adults in Clinton saw a new student like Robin, dressed like the kids in rap videos rather than the kids singing country songs, they tried to shield their children from what they regarded as his bad influence. Our school administration even cracked down on "gang culture."

After failing out of his first semester of college, Robin stayed close to the Clinton-Conway orbit, and he was twenty in 1995 when he met Darci at a house party in Clinton with some of her older friends. Robin had seen Darci, laughing and dancing, midriff bare, curly hair wild, and wanted to get to know her. She saw him, decided she liked him, and went over to talk to him. They danced, they made out. They found a quiet corner to smoke and talk about music, and she told him about her plan to move to California and take over the world with her talents and charm, becoming famous in some undetermined but predestined way. Soon they were dating.

When I met up with Robin as an adult, he told me he hadn't known how old Darci was until her sixteenth birthday the following spring, and when Virginia saw the shock on his face, she said, "It's okay!" Robin was also friends with Darci's brother, Cody, and often slept over instead of driving home. Soon Virginia invited Robin to stay indefinitely—he lived in a crowded trailer with three younger siblings in the middle of nowhere, and she thought she was helping him out. Officially, Robin was living with Cody, but all Darci's friends knew he slept in her room. At sixteen, Darci had a live-in boyfriend.

"She seemed older, so you wanted to treat her that way, but the reality is, she was just a baby," Robin recalled. Darci was so intelligent, so full of potential, and they had a great time partying. Robin's friend Dan Elliott, who hung out with them often, remembers Darci as smart and seemingly mature. Most of the other girls he knew in Clinton mainly tried to please boys, to make them like them, rather than join the conversation. But with Darci, he told me, "There was no joke, no obscure reference that went over her head." They talked about music and watched *Seinfeld*. "She just always knew what was up. She didn't give you a fake laugh to be part of the group. She knew what you were talking about." Darci was pretty, too, and had a good personality, but it was her intelligence, her independence, and her detachment from Clinton culture that struck Dan.

When I met Robin, he was the middle-aged father of two kids. In retrospect, he felt his relationship with Darci had been one of the most consequential of his life—she was the tragic love who broke his heart. "We were trying to survive," he told me, "and not be so bored. And drugs were always too easily accessible. But . . . we had no direction at that time. I think everybody that I hung out with, to a degree, seemed [to get] into a phase of being mischievous, acting out, doing stupid stuff."

Darci took muscle relaxers, Somas, recreationally, he told me. She'd been prescribed them in middle school, when we'd all been lined up to have an expert check our spines—a common practice in poor rural areas, where most people go without regular check-ups. Darci had left that quick consultation convinced she had scoliosis, a curved spine, though she'd never seemed to have back problems before. Virginia had dutifully taken her to the chiropractor, who had prescribed the Somas.

Darci took them throughout high school. Robin tried them, but they messed with him more than any other recreational drug he'd taken, and he didn't understand why Darci liked them so much. She once took so many that Virginia found her having what looked like a seizure in the bathtub. She accused Robin of letting her drink too much, but he said, "No, it's those pills she takes."

Robin had access to drugs—mostly pot and LSD—through his Conway skater friends. When Darci asked him to bring her some, as well as some beer if he could get it, he was happy to oblige. Once he pulled up to her house with the supplies she'd asked for, and he saw some other cars, including those driven by older men, pulling up, too, and he realized Darci was asking for drugs on behalf of some of her friends.

Darci's brother, Cody, who was two years ahead of us in school, had never been a good student. In his junior year, his grades weren't high enough to keep him on the football team, and he dropped out. Virginia had almost expected it—it was Darci she thought would go to college, though she hadn't articulated that expectation to Darci or set it out as a goal for her. Cody got jobs at various times, but he also hung out in the den with Darci, Robin, and anyone else who came by.

The den became a destination. People stayed there for hours and partied. Because Robin wore loose-fitting pants and listened to hip-hop and was part of a pothead crowd, people assumed he was a drug dealer. Hanging out in Darci's den, he realized he actually was.[*]

Early in Darci's sophomore year, her parents' house was raided. Police had called Virginia and asked to search the house for drugs, and she consented, but they found nothing and arrested no one. When I asked Darci about it years later, she said she'd hidden smiley face stickers laced with LSD inside a Bible, but none of the

---

[*] Robin was convicted of drug charges in 1995, for which he was put on probation. He later violated his probation and spent ninety days in jail.

officers had thought to look in her room. They'd come for Robin, the outsider who they'd already decided was a drug dealer.

No one suspected Darci of anything too bad, according to Virginia and others, because there were no obvious alarm bells. She was still earning A's in school. She had developed a talent for covering up emotional problems, keeping everything light, being the fun one, and making sure her mom didn't worry about her. She kept her drinking and drug use far out of sight of adults. Also, many adults in town considered older teenagers to also be adults already: after all, their own adult lives had started young, with early marriages and early parenthood. So local teenagers were often free to make their own choices, as if they were adults.

But other parents recognized that Darci had crossed the unspoken line between rowdy redneck and college-bound scholar. As "the right kind" of families ostracized her, she surrounded herself with older teenagers who spent their time partying.

6.

The Summer in New York

In 1999 a Columbia University graduate student in economics, Adriana Lleras-Muney, found that each additional year of education led to a longer life. It's a tight correlation—education is a stronger link to a longer life than even household income. Still, even a tight correlation doesn't mean the relationship is causal. Education "is also the thing that we measure about people the best," Lleras-Muney told me. "It is one of those things that we can collect data on. There could be other things that matter a lot more, but they're just very difficult to measure."

That idea has stayed with me. While we can divide education neatly into years and levels of achievement, students themselves are much harder to categorize and quantify. Why do some stay in school while others leave? The researchers asking that question are usually people with the highest levels of education, holding doctoral degrees. Occasionally, research uncovers some character trait that allows the most educated to succeed, both in their careers and in their lives. These explanations must be very tempting for people who see themselves on the winning side of that equation. But like all easy explanations, they're too neat; they can't grasp the fuller story.

. . .

In high school, I feared I only had two paths forward in life. One was to get stuck in Clinton and start having babies as soon as possible. The other was to go away to college. I didn't know many people, let alone daughters of plumbers, who went to college, stayed for four years, and graduated with a degree, except for my teachers. But I imagined college was my safest exit from Clinton.

When I was born, according to family lore, Daddy declared I would go to Harvard and become the first woman president. I don't know why—he often proclaimed he'd read only one book in his life, Stephen Crane's *The Red Badge of Courage*. Perhaps he was consoling himself that I wasn't a boy: if he had to have daughters—ultimately he would have three, and no sons—he wanted to believe we would become extraordinary women. My mom had always felt slighted by her family and by teachers who hadn't expected her to go to college, so she supported the Harvard dream for me. So did my mom's mom—one Christmas she brought me a fake Harvard sweatshirt, emblazoned with the school's crest and logo, from a dollar store. The fact that people shared the dream kept it from seeming like a delusion.

When I entered high school, I already had a reputation for being a smart kid. Our potential was set in middle school, and it determined how we approached our later years of education. The cliques at school could be vicious and tightly controlled—as I've said, the churchgoers, athletes, scholars, and popular kids were on one side, and the kids who partied on weekends were on the other. Sometimes your clique assignment was based on nothing more than someone's displeasure. When Vanessa's brother quit playing football, the coach forbade the other boys from hanging out with him. Susie, his mother, told me he was miserable, eating lunch alone in the cafeteria, hating school, hating Clinton, even long afterward.

The students whose parents had money were unquestionably

bound for college. For those of us without money, what we did in school hardly seemed to matter unless we excelled. A lot of adults would say to my peers. "What's the point of staying in school if you're miserable? Just get out, get your GED, and get on with life." I heard it a lot over the years: "If you're not making good grades, you're just wasting everyone's time." My friend Erica left high school at seventeen because she was offered a job as a manager at the local McDonald's. Her grades were not good. What was the point of staying, she thought, if she already had this good job lined up?

This kind of thinking extended beyond Clinton and beyond high school to become the question "What's the point of going to college if you don't know what you're going to do?" And over the years, as college expenses grew and scholarships became more competitive, the question morphed into a statement: "That's an awful lot of money to waste if you don't know what you're going to do." That's what my friend Paula Stapleton, who left the College of the Ozarks after two semesters, told me. People in Clinton still viewed college as the realm of the elite. For us, college first and foremost had to be a job-training program, since our biggest concern was money, both how much it would cost and how much we'd earn afterward. My family couldn't afford to pay tuition, so I knew I'd have to earn a scholarship. I didn't find out that wealthy, private, elite schools often handed out enormous financial aid packages to low-income students until I applied to those schools and received them myself.

Well before Darci and I turned sixteen, she and some of my other friends were already allowed to work late and to drive around at night and on weekends with friends. Many of their families bought them cars, even when it was a struggle financially. Cars are important in a spread-out rural county. Teenagers could get "hardship licenses" when they were as young as fourteen, which allowed them to drive alone, as long as their families attested to their need to get to school and to after-school jobs. To pay for gas, many of my friends started working late at fast-food places around town. Sonic paid especially well—minimum wage plus tips. In few other restaurants did diners routinely tip more than the change left over from a bill. The extra money gave my friends more freedom, and many spent it shopping in Conway, going to movies, or buying their own food—generally, entering adult life.

Ashley and I were never allowed to do any of this. Our parents wanted us to concentrate on school. They didn't want us to take on responsibilities like work and car payments, and they were strict about how we spent our free time and whom we spent it with. Instead of buying us a car, they built a house. Back in 1989, my dad had bought land from a friend for $14,000. He'd scrimped and saved to get a mortgage, then built much of the house on his own, acting as general contractor and calling in favors from friends. It was my parents' dream home, a two-story farmhouse with a wraparound porch, and it took more than a year to build. We moved in during the fall of 1994, in my freshman year of high school. Ashley was in the eighth grade, and Courtney was just starting middle school, and we each had our own room. It felt palatial, private, and quiet, even though we couldn't afford new furniture—for the first few months that we lived there, I slept on a pallet of blankets.

The new house was far from town, and from the windows, I could see trees extending forever, as if we were alone in the deep woods. Instead of passing cars the sounds that dominated were those of beavers splashing into the pond, birds, frogs, and wind. One weekend I started reading *Crime and Punishment,* which I'd found in my mom's Great Books set, leather-bound classics she'd ordered from a catalog early in her adulthood. *Crime and Punishment, Pride and Prejudice, Sense and Sensibility,* and *War and Peace* were all clumped together. I called them the "and" books and thought they were a set until I read them. The day I started reading *Crime and Punishment* in my new room, I heard a bird call and stood up to look out the windows at the trees across the street.

For much of my childhood, my mom was focused on building that house. I think I know why—she wanted to keep us safe from the travails of Clinton. A fortress. She wanted it to be nice enough that we would enjoy it and not seek fun elsewhere. And she wanted it to be far enough away from town that our friends would not stop by. She wanted us away from the judgment, the social pressure, the subtle class divisions, the boy craziness, the sneaking out at night that could make it hard for us to concentrate on going to college. She was determined to remove every distraction from our lives.

This was more of a battle in Ashley's case than in mine. Tall and skinny, teenage Ashley had grown out of her tomboy stage and now wore makeup. She kept her jet-black hair in a short, severe bob that accentuated the fey softness of her face. After my father died, I found a picture of him as a teenager, entering the army after boot camp, and he looked so much like Ashley, I had to catch my breath. In his final years, his drinking and work in the sun had made his face so bloated and red that I'd never seen Ashley in it, but she got her features from him. They had the same Cupid's bow lips, the same slightness, and the same ski-jump nose.

Ashley's style was unusual for Clinton, more alternative even than mine. She picked up clothes from thrift stores and pieced together weird, brightly colored outfits, featuring paisley pants that looked like old curtains and fake-leather jackets with an ineradicable musty smell. On one shopping trip, she found a pair of jazz pants—slim, shiny, black, and bell-bottomed—that she'd wear to practice routines from *All That Jazz* and *A Chorus Line*, dancing around the house, sleek and lithe. When she was about sixteen, she wore them for School Spirit Day, paired with a cropped top.

It was too much for Clinton—skintight pants, form-fitting top, on Ashley's model figure. A boy in her class shouted at her, "You make me sick!" because, he said, she looked too sexy. Later that day a cheerleader asked her to pretend to be a cat for a skit. Ashley just stood there, barely moving, saying "meow meow" half-heartedly. "I thought Ashley would really go for it!" her friend told me. But after her classmate shouted at her, Ashley probably didn't want to slink around on the gym floor in front of everyone in form-fitting pants. She was too much for Clinton in so many ways. Sometimes she wanted to make herself small and unnoticeable.

Once Ashley shoplifted from a local thrift store, probably just to see if she could. She was caught and had to return everything, but she was still prosecuted in juvenile court and sentenced to probation. Momma paid for her attorney and was more confused than angry. Who stole from a thrift store? Another time, when my dance class was in Missouri, to perform at a theme park, we went shopping at Walmart and heard a call over the loudspeaker: "Will Monica Potts and the Judi King dancers please come to the fitting rooms?" We ran over in a panic, convinced Ashley had tried to steal something. But she'd just asked an employee to page us. "I couldn't find you guys!" she said with faux innocence.

On another dance trip, we stayed overnight at a hotel in Memphis. My friends and I ordered porn on the hotel's TV, as a joke, and woke Ashley up to watch it. She'd gone to bed early and was upset that we'd awakened her. "Come on, I'm trying to be good!" she complained. She got up anyway and started making loud, crude jokes. As the night wore on, we got tired of our prank, but we couldn't wind Ashley back down. "You can't turn me on and off like a switch!" She stretched out languidly on the bed, her black bobbed hair spilling over her long, outstretched arm, but her eyes were electric, and I could almost see her brain trying to land on something new. She was tired, but we had started a game that she had trouble ending.

She took to stealing Momma's cigarettes and smoking when she thought the house was empty. I caught her once, and she claimed they helped her. Nicotine was one of her treatments for Tourette syndrome, after all. She painted her room black and drew pictures of crying teenage girls holding bottles of Evan Williams, a cheap whiskey. When we moved into the new house, my parents bought a knife block with green-handled knives. They started to go missing. I found them in Ashley's room, along with little cuts all over her thin ivory arms. Momma and Daddy took her to a psychologist, paid for by the new free health insurance program for children in the state, and consulted with doctors about her medications. She wanted to quit taking everything except the antidepressants, which she decided were necessary.

Once when Ashley was fifteen or sixteen, she went out with friends, a young couple who had had a baby together in tenth grade and kept dating. My parents probably allowed it because they assumed a couple with a newborn wouldn't get into trouble. But an hour or so after they left, they screeched back into the driveway in their big pickup truck. The young couple knocked on the door, crying, and rushed Daddy to the back seat. Ashley was there, nearly passed out. Daddy pulled her long, liquid body out, and we rushed her to the hospital.

There the doctor laughed and said Ashley was just intoxicated. She had alcohol poisoning. She kept saying, "It was a secret, it was a secret."

"I always thought that if something happened, at least I could save you with my big strong hands," Daddy told Ashley later, during a serious talk about her punishment. His own drinking was especially heavy by then, his face red and swollen and old, alcoholism eating away his health and youth. I worried about him constantly—that he'd have an accident driving drunk, that he'd have a heart attack—so his worries on Ashley's behalf carried an extra solemnity. "You just fell through my hands like water, baby."

The next day Momma and Daddy made her work her regular shift at the Sonic drive-in, hungover and miserable. This kind of behavior was Momma's worst nightmare—*What are we going to do to make sure Ashley gets out of here?* became her overriding concern.

• • •

When I took the ACT for practice in my sophomore year, I had to choose three colleges to send my scores to, even though I was still years from applying. "You should send them to Brinnaw or Brinna or something like that," my mom said from the kitchen as I filled in the little bubbles. "I don't know how to pronounce it, but it's where all the women writers go." She'd read the name in the "About the Author" section of some book jacket.

Much later I realized she meant Bryn Mawr, which was where I ended up going. At the time, though, I pored over the test's registration booklet, which had the codes for all the colleges we could send our scores to. Momma knew it was a women's college, so I filled in all the women's colleges I could find that started with a *B*, one of which was Barnard in New York. After I got my scores, Barnard's admissions office sent me a booklet that included an application. I thought it was nice, and ever the diligent student, I felt compelled to follow up with them in case they were expecting it back. I called the admissions office and thanked them for sending it but said I was only a sophomore and wasn't ready to apply for college yet.

Some weeks afterward, I received an application for Barnard's "Summer in New York," which it called a "pre-college program." I had never heard of such a thing, but it promised I would spend four weeks in the city taking college courses at Barnard to prepare for university-level learning. I decided to apply. I had a savings account with a little over a thousand dollars in it: my dad had saved his loose change over the years and divided it equally among us. I asked Daddy if I could use it for the New York program, if I got in, and he said yes absentmindedly, probably assuming they wouldn't admit me.

I did get in, but my scholarship was only eight hundred dollars. My bill would still total over two thousand dollars, which didn't even include the plane fare or the expenses of traveling to and from New York and living there. I called the office again and thanked them for admitting me but I wouldn't be able to go: I didn't have the money, and no one in town had money because we'd just gone through a scholarship race for students bound for actual college. The director of the summer program called back and said a grant was available for a low-income student to attend, and she'd decided I should have it because my essay had really touched her. I'd written about Ashley and her Tourette syndrome diagnosis.

The first flight I ever took was to LaGuardia Airport. My mom had gone to a travel agent and charged it on her credit card. She'd also arranged for a cab to pick me up and take me straight to Morningside Heights. I arrived on campus for the welcome picnic, wearing a ponytail and polo shirt from Walmart and jean shorts and sneakers. One girl said she had to run to a drugstore to buy a razor because she'd forgotten one. "By yourself!?!" I asked, incredulous that a teenager could be on her own in such a big city, and everyone just looked at me.

I was there for most of July and made friends from all over the country. People marveled at my accent and called it cute. I vowed to lose it, so that people would actually listen to what I had to say. My new friends and I roamed the city, seeing the Fifth Avenue shops and the World Trade Center and Central Park. We sat on benches in Battery Park and went to Barnes & Noble, "a famous bookstore," I recorded in my journal. We rode the subway everywhere. "Don't tell my parents they let us go out on our own," I confided in my journal, as if it were a person who would tattle or, more likely, as if Ashley or Courtney would read it. I saw the real difference between a city and the countryside, the massive crush of people, the money you could sense flowing through the streets. We toured the New York Stock Exchange, and I visited some of the country's oldest urban neighborhoods. There were entire worlds, I realized, that people in Clinton could pass their whole lives knowing nothing about.

We had opportunities to see Broadway plays, and everyone wanted to see *Rent*, which was still in its original cast that summer. I loved musicals but had only ever seen them in movies or with traveling casts in Little Rock or Memphis, so I really wanted to go, despite never having heard of *Rent*. Someone in the ticket line, who by chance had lived in Arkansas for a few years, did one of the kindest things anyone has ever done for me: she gave up her spot so I could have the last ticket to see *Rent* with my friends. "I know what it's like there, and you'll never have another chance to go," she said. As I watched the show, I decided I wanted the life it portrayed. I'd always been taught that the city was scary and people were cold, but to me it felt warm and welcoming, a place that accommodated difference, reveled in weirdness, and mostly left people alone to figure out what life they wanted. The city became a beacon to me, once I heard its big heartbeat—and before I got to know its more jagged edges.

I came back to Clinton grumpy and ready to live in New York forever. I also carried an evaluation from a professor who wrote of me, "She is just the kind of young woman I would like to see at Barnard again." The Barnard program had introduced me to a world of previously unknown colleges that my new friends told me about. I sensed I could get into them and do well in their classes. Most important, perhaps, it taught me that if I didn't have the money to attend, someone in an office somewhere might find it and give it to me. I kept that in mind when I applied to colleges a year later.

The Barnard program morphed my parents' boundless ambition for me into something more realistic. It helped me focus on school as a vehicle for leaving Clinton, even as the world I'd grown up in started to shift and challenge me. Whenever Clinton failed to accommodate my imagination, I now had an alternative world to rely on.

Yet my summer in New York had happened almost entirely by chance. Those elite pre-college summer programs are usually meant for the children of very wealthy parents who want to improve their chances of admission. I had heard about this one only because Momma had misread the name of a college on the back of a book jacket, because I'd happened to register for a college entrance exam early, because I'd followed up with a college that sent me promotional materials, and because I'd called the admissions office to say I couldn't afford it, not knowing I might have a chance of receiving financial aid. It felt so naïve and accidental, yet it changed my life, first and foremost by giving me something to look forward to over the next two years of high school.

What might Darci's life have been like if she'd had a similar experience? I wondered ever after. And what could our higher education landscape look like if all American students had access to similar experiences, preparing them for college and expanding their worlds?

7.

The Escape Plan

I was lonely and unhappy in my last two years of high school, especially after New York. I drifted away from all my friends. Maybe I walled myself off on purpose, to make it easier to leave, to make it almost impossible not to. In any case, I longed for an environment away from the people who knew me.

I handled the college application process on my own. My parents watched and listened and waited for updates. "Just tell us where you need to go, and we'll drive you there," my dad said, unsure about the whole endeavor but wanting to be supportive. Because of my trip to Barnard, I was on a mailing list for several universities, and at the beginning of my senior year I was swamped by brochures from colleges I'd never heard of, and a few big ones I had, like Princeton and Columbia. I requested materials from Harvard, but when it came down to it, I was too nervous to ask my teachers for recommendations for those Ivy League schools. A boy I briefly dated asked, "You don't really think you're going to get into a school like Harvard, do you?" He wasn't being mean, just honest. Applying to Harvard seemed as unrealistic as taking a trip to the moon. Would my teachers have the same skepticism? It would be embarrassing if I applied and didn't get in. Everyone would know about my foolish ambition. In the end, I didn't apply to any Ivy League schools.

I did apply to three schools in the state, two in Tennessee, and Barnard and Bryn Mawr, the school my mom had been trying to remember. They'd been welcoming and helpful, sending me materials and having students call me during the application process to see if I had any questions. Most of the Seven Sisters schools were in western Massachusetts, far from Boston, and I didn't want to be so far from a city. Bryn Mawr was only a train ride from Philadelphia and had a cooperative agreement with several surrounding schools, so I knew I wouldn't feel isolated. But I didn't think I'd really get in. I knew that Bryn Mawr and Barnard and Vanderbilt, the other top schools I applied to, would be much more expensive than the public colleges in Arkansas where I was expected to go.

I was awarded good scholarships from colleges around the state and accepted them all, unable to decide where I was going. I hoped I could figure it out before it was too late to get my deposits back, for which I'd used the money I earned from my job at Subway. Then in late spring, I got acceptance letters back from Barnard, Bryn Mawr, and Vanderbilt—with astounding financial aid packages. "They gave me everything I wanted," I wrote in my journal. "All because we're poor." My family's expected contribution in tuition, for all three schools, was only a couple thousand dollars, which I'd be able to pay from my work-study earnings in a monthly payment plan. They were giving me more aid than some of the private schools closer to home did. In the end, the money decided it. Other than the University of Arkansas, where I didn't really want to go, the schools with the highest price tags on paper were actually the cheapest for me to attend.

My mom wanted me to go to Vanderbilt, probably because Nashville was only a day's drive from home, and I could get back quickly if I needed to. Even my mom was nervous about me being too far out of her orbit—which I didn't know how to address since I'd thought I was fulfilling her biggest dream for me. She even tried to tempt me with a weekend visit to the Vanderbilt campus, but I knew I wanted to be close to New York and all that I remembered from my summer there. I worried Vanderbilt would be full of girls curling their hair and doing their makeup before football games, like other Southern girls I knew, because I hadn't experienced a South that was any different. I didn't want that life. I thought of my science teacher and his subtle sexism.

The women students who'd called me from Bryn Mawr to offer help were appealing to me in a way I didn't fully recognize—their confidence came through over the phone. Someone had told me that Bryn Mawr was a T-shirt and jeans kind of place, where students didn't dress to impress, and that it was academically rigorous. They thought I'd learn a lot there while also feeling at home. In contrast, Barnard was located in an expensive city, and I didn't know if I was ready for New York's frenetic energy. So Bryn Mawr, a school I never visited, felt right to me, easier than going to New York and closer to my imagined future.

It was still a fraught decision. I worried about being far from home and being able to get back quickly in an emergency. Alexandria Walton Radford, a sociologist who is now at the American Institutes for Research and studies why and how students make college decisions, told me that the middle- and upper-income high school students she interviewed almost never brought up the issue of nearness to home. But low-income students were accustomed both to family emergencies and to being part of their family's solution to them, a grown-up burden their wealthier counterparts did not have to bear. "I can talk nonchalantly about being away from home for months, but in real life I know better. I know I would get deathly homesick," I wrote in my journal. "I'll worry constantly."

I was specifically worried about my dad, whose health had declined even more. When I couldn't sleep, I would sometimes hear his coughing, which had always been bad but was now a hacking, wretched, whole-body spasm. He would cough late into the night, and sometimes I wished he'd have a minor heart attack to scare him into taking better care of himself. "I'm not stupid enough to deny the possibility that Daddy might die while I'm away," I wrote. "It's the thing we all dance around. . . . Daddy and the rest of us can't talk about lung cancer or emphysema."

At the same time, I knew, in some dreamy way, that Bryn Mawr was what I wanted. It felt like the kind of chance I'd stumbled into with Barnard. It was what my parents wanted for me, too, even if it made them nervous. "That's what they wanted when they told me the story about Daddy holding me after my birth and saying I would be the first woman president of the United States," I wrote in my journal.

It was a difficult decision to explain to people in Clinton. My principal, when I talked to him before graduation, didn't realize where I was going and kept referring to it as "down there," apparently thinking of colleges in Conway, and I didn't correct him. When I told my physics teacher I was going to a school outside Philadelphia, she exclaimed, "You'll regret it when there are bars on your windows!" To rural Arkansans, all cities are the same, and all are violent. Even my high school counselor, a chain-smoking, gray-moustached man who was always supportive, had no idea that private colleges gave out their own financial aid packages and was astounded that my expected contribution to Bryn Mawr was almost nothing. He'd always assumed that the wealthy colleges in the Northeast were financially out of reach for his students, so he'd forged no connections with them.

• • •

Almost everyone outside my family, and sometimes even my parents, seemed to subtly try to discourage me from going far away to college. The vast majority of people I knew went to nearby colleges—the University of Central Arkansas in Conway, less than an hour away; Arkansas State University in Jonesboro, close to Memphis; and the University of Arkansas in Fayetteville, a booming mountain town. Some went to nearby technical colleges, which later became junior colleges in the state systems. Many students made their decisions solely based on money; they'd spent high school trying to get the best grades and scores possible in order to snag state-based scholarships.

In 2019, curious to see if these attitudes persisted, I went to Clinton High School's graduation and met the class's valedictorian. Kiaura Balentine was a smart, thoughtful young woman. I asked her why she thought the valedictorian, the salutatorian, and the president of her class were all women. It's because girls knew they needed to go to college to have a chance at a good income, she told me: boys could enter a trade and work with their hands and still make more money than a teacher with a master's degree. Kiaura could probably get a bachelor's degree in nursing, she said, and still not make as much money as her high school boyfriend, who planned to go into heating and air after studying at the nearby community college: "It's going to take me four years to make, maybe, what he makes in the trade."

This is a fact. For the most part, women enter colleges at higher rates than men now because it's one way those on the lower end of the income scale can achieve parity with men. In Kiaura's world, jobs were strictly segregated by gender, and she never imagined that women could go into construction trades. "If anything had happened to my dad, my mom would be completely financially in need," she said. "There's no way she'd make enough money to support three children. . . . Receptionists . . . don't make the money men do." It's a conundrum. Schools treat girls differently, making their academic success harder to come by; at the same time, academic success is required for girls to succeed after they graduate. In the real world, the highest-achieving women are still being outcompeted by men, while the young women who stumble fall further behind than men with comparable academic performances.

Kiaura was born in Clinton after I left, to a family that had roots both in Illinois and the rural farming section of Van Buren County. Her dad worked in construction. She grew up in Formosa, a town even smaller than Clinton, and her grandfather had horses. She liked the country life. She had decided to go to Arkansas Technical University, primarily because the scholarship there was the highest, but also because it was close to home. I asked her if anyone in her class would have liked to go out of state for school, and she gave me Gisselle Hernandez's phone number.

Gisselle had been class president and dreamed of going to Vanderbilt because when she was in the eighth grade, her older brother—who had gone to the Arkansas School of Math, Sciences, and the Arts in Hot Springs—had gotten a brochure from the school. She'd asked him about Vanderbilt, and he'd said, "Oh, it's this prestigious school. It's very hard to get into. No one really gets in." She said, "I like difficult things. I like a challenge," and thereafter she developed a single-minded focus on getting into Vanderbilt.

Gisselle, whom I met in the summer of 2019, was friendly and sweet. She knew all the adults who entered our coffee shop and hugged and chatted with them all. She was petite, dark haired, and olive skinned. Her parents are from Mexico. She was part of a new generation of people in Van Buren County, Latino immigrants and their children, from Mexico and Central America. The county was still more than 90 percent white, but the Latino population had more than doubled, from just over 1 percent to more than 3 percent, in the years since I'd left. Many of the new residents worked in agriculture or the natural gas industry, and some families opened restaurants. In Clinton, many were connected to the Assembly of God church, the Pentecostal congregation, which had done missionary work throughout Mexico.

Gisselle was born in Arkansas and spoke with a Southern accent, which she thought put her in a weird position. The white Americans she grew up with tended to treat her as one of their own, but later she heard them say derogatory things about the Guatemalan immigrants who came to town. Her mother packed lunches for her, of rice and beans and fragrant, spicy meats, but she used to leave them in her cubby instead of taking them to the lunchroom because other kids thought the food was strange. Later her Mexican heritage became a source of pride, and she wrote her college admissions essays about the duality of growing up as a child of Latino immigrants in a small, rural Southern town.

In her senior year, she applied to Vanderbilt, the University of Arkansas at Little Rock, Arkansas State University, and the University of Arkansas Community College at Morrilton (UACCM,) the community college nearest Clinton, where many graduates went. Gisselle worried that Vanderbilt was a long shot.

From 2007 to 2009, I was a tutor for a test prep company, helping students with the SAT, and I also gave college advice. If I'd been Gisselle's tutor, I would have helped her find other colleges similar to Vanderbilt, with the same qualities she admired, and we would have devised an application strategy that included universities that might be easier to get into but were no less ambitious academically. And I would have made sure she applied for financial aid. No one did that for Gisselle. One of her teachers and mentors did encourage her to look at Baylor, a Baptist college in Texas, but Gisselle didn't like it, and that was the only other university anyone suggested. Gisselle took agriculture classes and was in Future Farmers of America, and those teachers told her to stay "in state and save money. They were just trying to be real with me." So she didn't look at any other out-of-state schools.

Gisselle didn't get into Vanderbilt. "You have to be a genius," she said sadly. Knowing of no comparable options, she applied to the University of Central Arkansas (UCA), but it was too late to get a scholarship. She'd missed the scholarship competition for many in-state schools. I spoke to her a few weeks before she started classes at UACCM, where she had a full scholarship. She hoped to transfer to UCA later. (She ultimately did.)

Gisselle worried people would judge her, because there's a stigma against community college, but that didn't happen. "I always dreamed of going to a four-year," she said. "It's not like I'm super hyped, as if I were going to Vanderbilt. But I'm excited in my own way about it. I'm excited to start learning and working toward what I want to do." She seemed to know what she wanted and what direction she was going in, so I told her she'd probably be okay.

She's focused and smart, and she probably will be okay. I don't think everyone should apply to Harvard or Bryn Mawr. I also believe that outcomes should be more equitable across institutions: students who attend Harvard shouldn't have better lives than those who attend a public university or a community college.*

---

* Overall, though, rates of community college completion are low. Before the Covid-19 pandemic, only 35 percent of community college students graduated, according to MDRC, a nonprofit social policy and educational research organization, compared with 60 percent of four-year students who completed a bachelor's degree within six years. Since community colleges disproportionately serve the nation's low-income students, this rate is alarming. A 2021 survey by the Association of Community College Trustees shows that community colleges identify uneven federal, state, and local funding as one of their biggest challenges, along with the fact that their students come with a range of unmet basic and mental health needs.

And Gisselle herself was set on her goals and more likely to overcome any challenges that first-time college students face.

Giselle's experience, attending a community college almost by accident, isn't that unusual for low-income and rural students. Low-income students are particularly prone to "undermatching," meaning academic achievers don't go to the most rigorous colleges that might otherwise have admitted them. Because the less rigorous colleges are less likely to serve their needs, they are more likely to drop out. Exactly how and why students end up at particular colleges is difficult to understand because universities guard most of that information closely. But an increasing amount of data over the years shows that the higher education system is exceedingly stratified socioeconomically, with the wealthiest students dominating at the most elite universities.

Something about college admissions and recruitment perpetuates inequalities in race, ethnicity, and class. In 2019 researchers at UCLA and the University of Arizona surveyed 140 colleges and found that they prefer to recruit from private schools and from neighborhoods where the median income is at least $100,000, which doesn't often describe rural areas. A decade ago Alexandria Walton Radford, then at Princeton University, studied why high school valedictorians chose to apply to certain colleges and how they did once they got there. She found that they tended to choose colleges based on their personal experience. Low-income students were at a disadvantage compared to their higher-income counterparts, even when their grades and scores were comparable. They tended to be like me: they knew few people who had gone far away to college, they were not recruited by those colleges, they received scant support from high school college counselors, and they were sometimes subtly discouraged. They didn't know about financial aid, and neither did their parents or counselors, so they didn't think they could afford private college tuition. The few who did apply got encouragement, as I did, from teachers who mentored them. Many of these students wanted to stay close to home in case of a family emergency. In general, they applied to fewer colleges than higher-income students did and tended to enroll in the public college or university nearest them.

These trends were likely exacerbated by the Covid-19 pandemic. Enrollment was down at colleges across the board, but especially at community colleges, where it dropped by 9.5 percent, according to the American Association of Community Colleges. When the physical campuses temporarily closed down, rural students who had left home to attend college found themselves back home with uneven broadband, struggling to keep up.

There's another factor that's difficult to measure, and therefore often missed, but critical: happiness. I was most likely happier at Bryn Mawr than I would have been at a state school in Arkansas. Students commit to spending four or more years of their lives at college, and it's important that they enjoy their time there and feel challenged both academically and socially in ways that tempt them to stay. It's almost impossible to measure what will make a particular student happy.

When I tutored upper-middle-class students in Connecticut in 2007 and 2009, I noticed that none of them worried about the geography or cost of college. They saw the entire country, and in some cases the world, as a landscape of opportunity available to them. But the students I knew back home were discouraged from thinking that way. In 2019 Walton Radford told me the big issue was inequities in information: low-income students and their families often did not know that even very elite private institutions might be within their reach. "Ultimately, it's the students' and the families' decision," she said. "But you don't want it to be based on not having sufficient information."

When Gisselle and I finished our interview at the coffee shop, I rushed off, not wanting her to see me cry. She'd summarized her application essay for me—describing her disorientation as a child of immigrant parents, at being part of two cultures, and her powerful ambivalence about Clinton—and all I could think was that if it had been my choice, I would have admitted her to any college. I was sad for her, not because she was going to community college but because she had gotten bad advice. Just at the moment when she had a life-changing decision to make and should have been dreaming big, the adults around her had encouraged her to dream small. It was one decision point in one person's life, but it had happened thousands upon thousands of times in low-income communities like mine, in thousands of tiny decisions.

Gisselle thought she had to stay in Arkansas because she didn't have money, and she thought she hadn't been admitted to Vanderbilt because she wasn't smart enough, but neither of those things was true, and she'd have known that if she'd had access to the resources that middle- and upper-income students take for granted. My community really was poor, not just in people's incomes but in the way their lack of money and experience trapped them in a tight echo chamber, allowing something untrue to become conventional wisdom. This kind of place will remain insular if people are discouraged from branching out, from trying new things. The people who do the discouraging think they're doing it for the good of the students, but they're giving them bad advice. This is how some small towns fail even their smartest, most ambitious kids.

And if Gisselle, the high school class president, an honor student, was so discouraged, what did that mean for the students who were doing less well, who didn't seek as much help from adults?

• • •

Darci's life might have been different if she'd been channeled more successfully into an escape plan that excited her, I often thought in later years. But as it was, she concluded that college was just a job training mill and started to reject the idea. "People are so worried about money and success," she'd muse. "I just think it's important to be happy." It says something about the world she knew that she saw those two things as irreconcilable. I'd later meet people who went to hippie schools and studied weird things and smoked pot and didn't get grades. Others went to schools that expanded their minds and allowed them to challenge and question authority, which is what many people think college is for.

Darci thought that if she went to college, it would be UCA and that afterward she'd probably return to Clinton and be a teacher. It was a great future for those who wanted it, but it wasn't what she wanted, and she didn't have a model for going to college that would lead to a different future. The idea that you could support yourself as a journalist or artist or writer didn't even occur to her, or to me. Darci's postcollege future felt like a letdown even before she finished high school.

Darci was too interested in partying to focus on school, Robin and others told me. But why was she partying? Why was she diverted, and why did she go from being one of the best students in school to leaving without a diploma? Since education is a strong determinant of life expectancy, many policy makers focus on ways that ensure people stay in school for as long as possible. Is the key to solving the problem of deaths of despair to keep students enrolled until they finish college? Some people believe a college education is the solution to income inequality, to the shifting and changing job market, and to intergenerational poverty. For them, education is the solution to almost every problem. But what about students who struggle in school?

Why do some people do well in formal education settings while others don't? In the 1970s, the Stanford psychologist Walter Mischel devised a test to see how patient children could be if they were promised a reward for waiting. He put a marshmallow in front of four- and five-year-olds and challenged them to not eat it: if they waited fifteen minutes and didn't eat the marshmallow in front of them, they would be rewarded with two marshmallows to eat. The researchers recorded the children's responses, then followed them throughout their lives. The follow-up studies found a link between how long the children had been able to wait for the marshmallow and their success, as measured by educational and health outcomes, later in life.

The researchers may never have intended their findings to be prescriptive, but the idea of a "marshmallow test" took off nevertheless. It inspired a host of research into how character traits can influence educational attainment and success. Charter schools like KIPP started to teach self-control and emphasize personality attributes like "grit," "self-control," and "gratitude." Such "character education" became the focus of the charter school movement, which has educated an entire generation of students. In 2006 the *New York Times* columnist David Brooks wrote, "If you're a policy maker and you are not talking about core psychological traits like delayed gratification skills, then you're just dancing around with proxy issues."

Unfortunately the original study was very limited: the researchers recruited children from Stanford's nursery school, so the sample was small and consisted mostly of wealthy children of well-educated parents. As a graduate student, Tyler Watts, who is now a developmental psychology professor at Teachers College, Columbia University, decided to compare the results of the marshmallow test to other factors. He and colleagues found a large data set from a study conducted by the National Institutes of Health, beginning in the 1990s, that looked at nearly a thousand children.

The researchers had given four-year-olds the marshmallow test, but they had also studied many other things about the children over time, like their parents' income level, their mothers' educational attainment, the presence of books in their homes, and less obviously, the frequency of their parents' interactions with them and the quality of those interactions. These measures are standard in sociology and are used to assess the structural barriers families face as well as socioeconomic and cultural differences. When Watts and his colleagues controlled for all these other measures, they found that children's ability to delay gratification—the character trait measured by the marshmallow test—hardly mattered at all. Whether a child could wait to eat a marshmallow didn't determine how well they did in school or later in life. Rather, their ability to delay gratification was more a symptom of everything else influencing their lives than some all-important quality that would allow them to overcome all obstacles.

I asked Watts why he thought the original study had become so ubiquitous. "I think in the education policy world, and in the intervention world, even though no one will say this, we're often looking for silver bullets," he said. "We want to believe that there's some intervention out there that's very cheap, that's very easy, and that we can implement that will then have this kind of outsize effect on a kid's life."

This is especially true in the education policy community, which every day faces depressing data about gaps in education based on socioeconomic status, race, ethnicity, and gender. Many of these researchers and policy makers care about inequality, and they want education to solve it. "What I'm starting to think is more likely the case," Watts said, "is that all of the things that are leading someone to be disadvantaged are complex, and they're sometimes multigenerational, and they're embedded in both the culture and the environment and personal behavior. In order to

8.

Trauma

When I returned to my hometown as an adult, older adults who had known me as a child told me things—gossip, confessions—that they never would have told me as a child. Vanessa's mom, Susie, told me she'd been molested when she was about thirteen. "Most girls were," she said casually. "Half of Clinton. Christian, non-Christian, hillbilly, hick, a lot of girls it happened to. It was one of the closet secrets."

To get out of that situation, while she was still young, she'd married a Christian man. In the beginning of their marriage, she told me, they were so strict about traditional observances that she'd walked ten paces behind her husband. To me, that helped explain why she'd encouraged Vanessa to move to Colorado and get married at fifteen. It was how Susie herself had escaped.

Susie was describing a population, it turned out, that was living with unresolved trauma. Stories emerged everywhere of abusive parents and husbands, of sexual abuse, of neglect and poverty. For much of the time I was growing up, the town lacked mental health care, missing enough social workers or others who might have helped children facing abuse. These insular religious communities tried to resolve their problems in pastors' offices, in private—and some were surely told, as my friend April was, to pray for their abusive boyfriends or husbands.

Susie was also right that people didn't talk about these problems directly, though rumors always flew everywhere. She herself had always tried to be up front about her own family's problems, though her honest accounting had been used against her, she thought. Other parents had used her honesty as ammunition to blame Vanessa when their own daughters started acting out. Susie readily admitted it when Vanessa got out of line. "You as a parent, when you stick your head in the sand and don't take action when they're young enough [for you] to take action, to beat the dog out of them or ground them or scare them, by the time they're fifteen and sixteen it's too late," she said.

People in Clinton did bury their heads in the sand to avoid being judged, but many of the problems there—both in individual families and in the community as a whole—were, I could see now, just too big to handle. Few people or institutions had the resources to deal with any of them or to fix the biggest issues. Only after I went home again did I understand how exhausting it could be to push against a whole town's worth of trouble—the widespread poverty, the lack of social institutions, the abuse hidden in isolated homes. Rather than face certain defeat, people gave up and tried to preserve whatever they had left.

• • •

On a visit home in 2017, I asked Virginia about her own childhood. What had it been like for her to grow up in Clinton? Sitting at her kitchen table, she talked in the matter-of-fact way my dad often had: much of what she said was sad, but she didn't seem saddened by it. Her life was just there, a fact, and the events she related had happened long before.

Virginia grew up in Illinois, with two older sisters from her mom's first marriage, and three younger siblings. The two older sisters had married brothers from Van Buren County, Arkansas, and they both moved down here to start their families. When Virginia was a teenager, her mom went to Arkansas to visit them and met a new man. She divorced Virginia's dad, left him behind in Illinois, and married the Arkansas man, who became her third husband. She moved her whole family here.

Of her stepfather, Virginia said, "He was not a good guy," and waved her hand and shook her head at me. He was controlling and paranoid. "Drugs wasn't in the picture, there was something wrong with his mind. [Mom] was his fifth wife." Virginia shook her head again. This was part of him not being a good guy, I realized.

They all lived on the Mountain, north of town, near an old sawmill, down a trail road that hardly exists anymore. They didn't have a house—"it was like a tent and a really old camper thing, no running water, or anything, very primitive," she said. Virginia and her younger brothers had to walk to a neighbor's house about a mile away to get water from their well, or they went without water.

Virginia's two older sisters, who lived nearby, complained to the sheriff about their living conditions, but he said he couldn't do anything. Then Virginia's mom and stepdad went on a vacation, leaving Virginia and her younger siblings behind. The two sisters took the opportunity to bring the kids to live with them. One night at midnight, they drove to the Mountain, parked their cars on the edge of the highway, ran through the forest, down the old trail road, and reached the tent where Virginia and her siblings were living.

Virginia, who was about sixteen, and her siblings hadn't known their two sisters were coming. Suddenly, they saw flashlights shining through the canvas in the night. "We didn't know who it was at first," she told me. "They said, 'Get your stuff together and we're taking you.' And we didn't have a lot of stuff. We didn't argue. We got all our things and we were out of there."

It was a rescue, and everyone was relieved. Virginia and her siblings hadn't been happy there. The two older sisters split the younger ones up between them and received legal guardianship, so the kids never had to return to the tent on the Mountain. As an adult, I'd heard similar, and worse, stories from other friends' moms. That kind of neglect was common in Clinton then, but stayed in the background, the kind of family business that was never discussed.

Virginia was seventeen when her sister got custody of her, and a short while later she met Darci's dad, Dennis. Did you ever think of going to college? I asked her. She said she'd thought of being a teacher, or a nurse, like her mom, but they weren't priorities. "Your goal, a lot of times, you wanted to find a good guy and get married and have kids and have a nice home and have a good life," she said. "If you had a job, yeah that would be okay, but having a job, a career, whatever, was not a top priority. For me and a lot of my friends." Some girls in her class did go to college, but it wasn't the norm.

When Virginia met Dennis, he had a good job with the electric company, and his own car. "There were some guys that didn't have vehicles, they had no jobs, and that didn't appeal to me," she said.

"No more tents!" I said, and we laughed, awkwardly.

It made sense to me now that Virginia had always sought peace and comfort and avoided conflict. Like Susie, she was worried primarily about her children eating enough, being physically safe, and having a home. How confusing it must have been for them, for all our moms, that once those things were provided, once those basic needs were satisfied, it still wasn't enough. Darci was safe and cared for, but she'd still needed more, and Virginia, whose own childhood trauma lay just below the surface, who'd always worked hard to keep her children happy, had never been able to figure out what more she could do.

. . .

What was my own mom's damage? I wondered. When I was about fourteen and we were moving to the newly built house, I finally opened her forbidden trunk, the one from her Chicago life, at the foot of her bed. It didn't have a lock, just a button that looked like a lock, and all I had to do to satisfy my curiosity and invade my mom's deepest privacy was push it. Inside, I found a cup shaped like a cowboy boot, some other little toys, and a faded picture of a boy, about four years old, in a flannel shirt, smiling into the camera.

I asked my mom about it, as we were sitting on the patio, next to the path where Darci and I and my sisters had played for so many years. She told me the boy was her son, Brian. He'd had an accident when he was four and died of the head injury. That was it. She didn't want to talk about it anymore, or ever again.

My mom had been married before she met my dad—that I'd learned by the time I was a teenager—and that marriage was why she'd moved to Chicago. When I learned about Brian, I assumed he had been her son from her first marriage. But on one of my visits home in 2018, when I cautiously brought up the subject of Brian and her first marriage, she surprised me, saying, "Oh, he wasn't even his kid."

We were sitting in her living room while she played Candy Crush on her phone, and I was annoying her with questions about her life. "Who was his dad?" I asked, laughing nervously.

"Oh, some boy." Momma confessed that when she was a teen-ager in the 1960s, she'd partied at the Narrows, a spot on the lake where kids went and drank beer and had sex in cars. She'd had the baby during what should have been her last year of high school. That was why she wasn't among the graduates in the senior class picture from 1968 that hung in the hallway at the high school, and why, when I asked her if she'd graduated high school, she'd always said dismissively, "Oh, yes, through paperwork." She'd had her child and lived in a crowded little shack with her conservative Catholic parents and younger siblings. She'd married the man who took her to Illinois, both because he'd agreed to marry her and accept her son and because her parents wanted her to. "That's just what you did back then," she said.

Anguish passed over her face, but then she locked it up again, hands clasped, mouth squeezed tight, and went back to the game on her phone. She didn't talk more about it. I knew she'd left the marriage and returned home to Clinton. She met my dad here when she was in her late twenties. But she had spent some of the years between her son's death and my birth living singly in Chicago, struggling, and not wanting to come home because it would have meant admitting failure. She had told me, long before, that she'd spent her first night back in Arkansas alone in an old house in the holler, a tiny shack her parents had once lived in. She'd heard a whip-poor-will cry and starting sobbing.

She had been a teen mom, rushed into a terrible marriage, survived, and then found my dad who, despite the drinking problem, was mostly good and hardworking. He had a big heart and would be proud of his children and on board with her plans for them. "I think I had become so unmoored from all the other stuff, that he just kind of moored me," she said of Daddy. "Does that make sense? Because he was calm and placid, and he wouldn't fight, you know what I'm saying? That meant a lot, to not feel any of that whatever I guess that other was. And he was just comfortable for me to be around. That sounds so awful."

It turns out that Virginia, early in her marriage to Darci's dad, had also had a child, a son, who'd died young, from an infection that started in his ear. Darci had found out about him by sneaking around. When she was a teenager, she opened an old journal of her mom's, in which Virginia had written messages to God, wondering how it could have happened, what her son's death meant, what could have been done to prevent it. Darci thought that was probably why Virginia was so quick to take them to the doctor when something was wrong with them. Infant mortality is still higher in rural areas than elsewhere: people lose children, people are lost as children, and no one ever talks about it. Women often bear the pain silently.

My mom, Darci's mom, Vanessa's mom, and many other friends' moms—they'd all been seeking a safe harbor. Raising us, they had tried to avoid seeing us repeat their own mistakes, or they tried to solve our problems in the ways they knew how. A relatively new, controversial field of psychology studies transgenerational trauma, the idea that the pain from a traumatic event can be passed through generations. The children and grandchildren of Holocaust survivors, for example, sought psychological care at higher rates than their peers. Black Americans are affected by the oppression and racism experienced not just in their own lives but also in the lives of their parents and grandparents. More finite traumas can also be passed down within families and in communities where tragedies are common, in poor towns like mine where survival can seem to require an unwinnable battle; the exhausting repetition of the same bad things happening to your family and your neighbors again and again, over the years.

In 2019 the Centers for Disease Control found that Arkansas has the highest rate of childhood trauma, with 56 percent of its children experiencing at least one devastating event. Our rural Arkansas culture has limited tools for dealing with traumas—people

9.

The Goodbye

Darci had her own share of trauma in high school. Robin filled me in on what I hadn't seen, or hadn't wanted to see, during the years when she and I had drifted apart. My response to her situation at the time had been selfish—we had a huge fight, and it was my fault.

When Darci was about eight, Virginia and Dennis hit a roadblock in their marriage. Darci went to bed one night and heard them arguing in the living room. Her mom started crying. Darci came out and asked what was wrong, and Virginia said tearfully, "Your father doesn't love us anymore."

Dennis, it turned out, was having an affair. After that night, he and Virginia divorced. For the next year, Darci and Cody visited their father and his girlfriend in Fairfield Bay, about twenty minutes from Clinton, for pizza and ice cream and forced fun. Before the divorce, Darci remembered, she and her dad used to go fishing in the river together, but after he left, they didn't.

Virginia began working as a bookkeeper, took up walking for exercise, and lost weight.

After about a year, Dennis's relationship crumbled, and he and Virginia remarried. In a photo of their second wedding that Darci once showed me, Dennis and Virginia are holding each other and smiling big. Darci is sitting in the background in a blue dress, her hair still puffy, like it was throughout her childhood. She's grinning shyly, looking at her parents sideways. "I look like I'm saying, 'I don't know about this, guys,'" she told me later, laughing.

I had known about the divorce, but Darci's house, and our friendship, stayed mostly the same, and I never thought about it. Then in her freshman year, Dennis strayed again. Darci shared her first class of the school day, an English class, with Crystal, the daughter of the woman her dad was having an affair with. Every morning Crystal greeted Darci crowing about her mother's affair with Darci's dad, saying things like "Your dad had a fun time with my mom last night!" And Darci knew it was true. Her dad had been leaving for work early and coming home late. Because of Crystal, Darci and Cody found out about the affair before their mom did.

The second divorce happened so fast I barely registered it. In what felt like a matter of days, Darci's dad was gone from her life again.* For many years after the second divorce, Darci didn't speak to her father, she told me, and I remember feeling her dad's total absence afterward, like he'd just disappeared.

Virginia soon married another man who'd been a neighbor and friend. He moved in, and Darci suddenly had a new stepdad. Confusingly, his name was also Dennis. "Dennis was sleeping all the time," Robin, who was living with them, remembered. "The only time he was ever awake was to send us to get alcohol." Because our county was dry, he would give Robin and Cody cash to drive to Center Ridge, on the other side of the county line, about twenty minutes away, where people would go to buy beer at the liquor store in the middle of nowhere. "He was always sleeping in the

---

* I tracked down Darci's dad and stepmom later, as an adult, but neither agreed to be interviewed by me.

fetal position. It was real scary stuff," Robin said. "He was a pill head. He was always taking pills. We never knew what the pills were."

This second Dennis, Robin told me, had a heart condition. One day Dennis was in his room asleep, and Robin had a weird feeling that something was wrong, but he didn't want to check. Second Dennis's son from his previous marriage, who was just eleven or twelve, came over to the house, walked into the bedroom, and found his father lying unresponsive. "He started screaming, 'Oh my God, my dad is dead, my dad is dead,'" Robin said. "If I would have had the courage, I could have been the one to find him. The reality is, my worst fear was that he was dead. It really messed with all of us. We were all so powerless." Virginia had been married to him for just a few months.

He died in the fall of 1995, at the beginning of our sophomore year. We were supposed to travel to Nashville for a dance trip, but because her stepfather had just died, Darci decided not to go. I was furious. She and I were still close, but I was often angry at her—she was quitting so many things, partying with older kids, missing school, and acting out. I don't remember the details, but for some reason the fact that she wasn't going meant that I wouldn't be able to go. Her loyalties had slowly and steadily shifted so that she'd stopped fulfilling her promises not only to our dance group and to her school but to me.

Her announcement that she couldn't go because her stepdad had died left me cold. I had barely processed that she had a stepdad, and I'm not sure I had the emotional maturity to think about everything that had happened to her: her parents' divorce, her estrangement from her father, the addition and quick subtraction of a stepfather. Instead, I said to her something like "Well, it's not like your mom was married to him for that long."

Darci screwed up her face, put her head into the wall in the school's hallway, and sobbed. Even while we were talking, her eyes had been red, and she'd already been crying. If I'd noticed, I might have thought harder about what to say and reconsidered my anger, my smaller drama. But I didn't.

"He was a family friend!" she protested. "I knew him for a long time before my mom married him."

One of her older friends had seen our interaction and came over to rescue Darci from me. "Anyone who says that to you is not your friend," the girl said. They turned their backs to me and walked away together. Darci and I later made up, but things between us were strained for some time.

After her second husband's death, on Valentine's Day 1997, Virginia married a man called David. Darci thought it was what her mom needed to deal with her sadness, but she also felt abandoned and rejected. In retrospect, Darci's parents' divorces were clearly traumatic for her. But she had to deal with her feelings alone. She only told me about her sense of abandonment later, and she hadn't shared it with her other friends.

When I met up with Virginia again, I asked her if Darci had ever told her about her feelings of abandonment. She said she had, and Virginia had encouraged her to talk to Dennis. "Not to be rude, but it was his fault," she said. She didn't think Darci had ever spoken to him about the divorces, about his leaving. "At some point, she's just going to have to get over it," Virginia said to me.

The summer after Virginia's marriage to David, Darci went on what was meant to be our California trip without me, piling into someone's car with her older friends and starting down the road without much of a plan. Somewhere in New Mexico, she took pictures of herself next to a Historic Route 66 marker, her curly dark hair blowing in the wind, throwing up a peace sign with her two fingers. But they never made it to California. They ran out of money and had to turn around and come back to Clinton and their summer jobs.

When I met up with Darci again as an adult, she pointed to this time in her life, between ages fifteen and seventeen, as critical. While she admitted she was rebellious and would have done what she wanted regardless, she also said she might have been steered in a different direction. Her stepdad David tried to be a disciplinarian with Darci and Cody, but it didn't work. They liked him, but they didn't accept him as an authority figure.

Her parents' divorces and her mom's quick remarriages would echo through the choices Darci made—about men, about school, about family, about what to tolerate from others and how to process pain—both at the time and later in her life. Soon afterward she stopped coming to school. Virginia was too preoccupied with her problems to push her to go back. Darci has never wanted to blame her mother for everything that happened to her, but she has come to feel that, especially in the period following her second divorce, Virginia failed to discipline her or Cody in an effort to avoid conflict.

I don't know why Virginia married and remarried so quickly, but I do know that she, like many women in Clinton, could not really conceive of a single life. Women in Clinton relied on men. Virginia needed a husband, both spiritually and financially, and she needed to be a wife, and to be thought of as a good mother. "Now, me and Dennis [Darci's dad] had our own thing going on," she said once, referring to their divorce, admitting to being distracted. Her and Dennis's problems consumed them to the point that neither had the emotional space to help their children deal with divorce. Virginia viewed her divorces in terms of her own devastation and as none of her children's concern. She remarried to create a safe harbor for herself.

• • •

In our senior year, Darci had a new boyfriend, the son of hippie back-to-the-landers who lived on a mountain west of town, in a small community, hardly a town at all, called Alread. Then she became pregnant. She didn't want the baby, but abortion was never discussed as an option when we were growing up, not publicly anyway. She miscarried, still in her first trimester, in January 1998, toward the end of senior year. She went to an ob-gyn clinic in Conway for aftercare, and they gave her a note saying she should take a week off school because of an unspecified illness.

Darci's relief was overwhelming, but she kept it all to herself, the relief, worry, and whatever sadness. I didn't know her boyfriend or that she'd been pregnant and had a miscarriage. None of her other friends knew, not even the boyfriend. She just drifted away from him and stopped seeing him.

This was a turning point for Darci: she decided she would deal with her troubles on her own without seeking help, even if she needed it. Part of her didn't want to admit that she was struggling in any way; she still wanted to seem capable, bright, competent, adult. And part of it had to do with the complicated ways the town viewed teen pregnancy. It was as if the town's worst traits—religious judgment, disapproval of the girls who went boy crazy, lack of sexual education, and low expectations for girls overall—had crystallized in her pregnancy and then quietly buried themselves within her body, a weight to carry for the rest of her life.

While Darci was going through all this, during our final semester of high school, I was already checked out. Because our school was small and didn't offer many electives, many juniors finished all their necessary credits and went to college early. After the cheerleading season ended, I ran out of classes to take—I had three empty periods in a row. With nothing to do, I was bored. I would go into the nurse's office, complain of a stomachache, and take a nap on the medical table in the quiet, windowless room. Because I was a good student, I was allowed the naps and the lazy attitude. My only goal was to become the class's valedictorian, and I was competing against only one other student. I focused on not making a B in physics, which I'd jumped into halfway through the year.

In our senior year, students who were unlikely to graduate were often quietly ushered out of school altogether. In most cases they didn't have time to rectify their high school credit issues, so the principal and teachers met with parents and students and told them it was too late. A friend of my mom's got angry at the principal for not notifying her of her son's problems sooner, but the principal replied that, since her son was eighteen, whether to come to class was his decision.

As for Darci, even with all her partying and absences, she had the grades and ACT scores to get a scholarship at most state schools. It didn't feel like she needed to be at Clinton High School at all, so she stopped coming altogether. After her miscarriage, every time she missed a day of school, she whited out the excuse letter she'd gotten from the ob-gyn and wrote in a new date. Darci had used letters like this to skip school in previous years, too, but not as frequently. She had always done whatever she wanted and had always gotten away with it—it had always emboldened her to try to get away with even more. But by this time, I was so absorbed in my own life, I hardly noticed.

Kasey Kimmons, whose parents had been my family's landlords in the Shirley trailer, was hanging out with Darci all the time. Darci let Kasey use her doctor's note, too, and they stayed in her den and smoked pot and soon tried crystal meth. Darci was still working as a carhop at the Sonic, and people sometimes gave her meth as a tip. Meth was always around. It was easier to get than alcohol.

It didn't seem to matter to anyone that Darci and Kasey weren't in school. Then one day in April, near the end of the school year, a teacher caught Kasey in the hallway. "I know what you've been doing, and it stops now!"

Kasey was terrified. Both girls were pulled into the principal's office. They had missed seventy-eight days that year, they were told, and could not graduate. There was nothing they could do about it. They could walk with our class at the graduation ceremony, for the satisfaction of participating in the ritual and getting their pictures taken in a cap and gown, for their parents' sake. But even to be able to do that, they would have to show up for the twenty-two days that remained in the school year, and they would be given a fake diploma. Alternatively, they could return to school the following year or work toward a GED.

"What does it matter if I'm there or not!" Darci screamed at the principal, Mr. Hutto, slamming her hands on his desk. Her grades were still good. Obviously she didn't need to show up to class if she could excel without doing so, she thought. She had already been accepted into colleges with scholarships. The end of school seemed like a farce to Darci, so she stalked out.

Kasey's parents, mortified and furious, forced her to go to school every day, and Kasey did walk with the class at graduation. But Darci did not. None of the adults responsible for her, her parents or stepparents—her dad had married Crystal's mom by then—intervened and made her continue going to school so that she could walk in her graduation ceremony. In fact, she didn't show up at all. I got what I wanted and gave the valedictory address that night on the football field, but Darci wasn't there.

In 2017 I reconnected with Mr. Hutto and asked him about

Darci. We talked about her for some time. He'd always liked her, he said. She was kind and thoughtful and nice to everyone.

I told him I was writing about what happened to her during senior year.

He looked confused. "What happened to her?"

I recounted the story she'd told me, about how she'd been kicked out of school and treated so unfairly. All the adults had been so punitive to such a good student, and I'd shared her anger ever since.

Mr. Hutto's face showed surprise, and he said he didn't remember it.

Why had he kicked her out of high school right before graduation? I asked.

"I would have followed whatever was in the rule book," he said very sincerely.

Only later did I realize what Mr. Hutto was saying. The reason Darci hadn't finished school was that she'd missed too many days. She hadn't met the qualifications. The state laid out rules for earning a diploma, and Darci hadn't met them. The adults had enforced the rules.

What was legitimately angering about it was that no one had stopped Darci before that point. Whose job had it been to notice that she and her friend were skipping school using a transparent ruse? Shouldn't the principal or teachers have seen what was happening and stepped in before she'd missed too many days to save her diploma? Shouldn't Virginia have? Or maybe I, her good friend who'd seen her spinning out of control and planned to say something but never did, could have done something. Maybe I was the one who could have altered Darci's course.

It shouldn't really have mattered whether Darci finished school. Not having a diploma wouldn't have changed her college acceptance and scholarships, and she could have walked away from

Clinton nearly in the same position she would have been in if she'd actually gotten a diploma.

For Darci, though, it had been devastating. Her luck had run out at the worst possible time. She'd broken rules for so long. It was the first time she'd really faced any consequences, and they were unexpectedly severe. Worse for her, though, was that she'd always thought she was smart, she'd always done well in school, and leaving without a diploma caused an identity crisis. She started to apply for jobs, and when she had to check a box in the application indicating whether she had a high school diploma, she didn't know what to do. Sometimes she'd check "other" and write a long explanation about how she'd really graduated from high school even though she technically hadn't.

Not graduating from high school left Darci adrift in an adult life she wasn't quite prepared for. Equally wounding was the fact that Darci's parents had allowed it to happen. Darci could never get Virginia to push back at her, to make her do things, to *try*, and that had the counterintuitive effect of sapping Darci's fight. It made Darci harder, more skeptical, and less amenable to taking advice. She'd always done what she wanted, and now that was even more true.

When I resumed contact with her, the fact that she hadn't finished high school with me was the biggest gap between us. It put her into one demographic group, and me in another.

Of course, our lives had differed in many ways even before that point, but those ways were hard or impossible to quantify, the kind that don't pop up on statistical measures. People might point to her outward behavior and try to attribute it to some fundamental character trait. The family turmoil, the miscarriage, the social isolation from kids her age as they pulled away from her because of the bright line that increasingly separated them: it would be easy for no one to ever know all that, or to reckon with it.

• • •

Momma worked hard to find an outlet for Ashley, a way for her to feel good about herself. So did everyone else who loved her. At the end of her sophomore year, our dance school put on a re-creation of "Thriller" and chose Ashley to play Michael Jackson. The rest of us were the zombies. For weeks we practiced the dance around Ashley, who was choreographing her own routine and didn't want to show us before she was ready. She would just stand there as we danced, marking time, bobbling her head. She practiced alone in her room, watching a compilation of Michael Jackson videos, not just "Thriller" but also "Beat It" and "Bad." Ashley was athletic and had a malleable body that could move like Jackson's. She'd been moonwalking since we were children, and she wore a single pink mitten the way he wore a sparkling glove during his Motown 25 performance of "Billie Jean." No one had any doubt she could do it.

The question was whether she would. Ashley was a perfection-ist. She wasn't going to do something unless she thought she was ready. Since the first time she'd protested a dance she didn't like by not doing it when she was four, she knew she could thwart expectations, refusing to conform to other people's desires for her, and it gave her a kind of power. She had control over so little; at times she couldn't even control her own body. She took a kind of glee in sabotaging others' plans, in ways that could be dramatic but frustrating for the rest of us.

We didn't see her solo before the first performance. It was in a nearby town where our teacher had a second dance school. We drove an hour to get there. The costume designer had stitched a red leather jacket for her, and she wore red pants, white socks, and black penny loafers.

The lights went off for the beginning of the dance, and the rest of us tried to emerge spookily from the fake gravestones. The spotlight fell on Ashley, and her hand shot up into the air. Then she moved around the dance floor like liquid. Everyone screamed. I stopped, unable to keep dancing, just watching her.

Love for Michael Jackson had always seemed like something particular to Ashley, who had a poster of him with a white panther on her wall. Ashley, who was so different from the rest of Clinton, could make any movie or piece of music or dance or global pop star feel like her very own.

That summer Momma talked Ashley into applying to a free educational camp like the ones I'd always gone to. She was accepted to one called SummerStage. There she was cast as the First Witch in a condensed stage version of *Macbeth*, which would be part of a larger end-of-camp program.

She was away from home for three weeks. We knew she was having a good time, but we didn't know what to expect when we went to see her performance. She came out onto the stage and talked in a gnarly, mangled voice, loud and clear, sounding exactly like a witch. She captivated the room. Momma grabbed my hand. During an interval, we heard someone asking their child who the First Witch was. "My daughter!" Daddy interjected proudly.

Later, the director of the arts program at Lyon College, the liberal arts college that hosted the camp, sent my parents a letter and told them he'd encouraged Ashley to apply, that he'd love to see her attend college there. He wrote that she'd seemed surprised, and that he'd told her small towns could be hard on artistic kids. Everything changes when you leave, he'd promised her.

• • •

As the oldest kid in my family, I was the first to learn to drive. When I was seventeen, at the beginning of my senior year, my dad found a good deal on a 1988 Ford Tempo and the money to buy it, in the way that only he could. I had a car, but it was really "the kids' car." I used it to ferry my sisters around. And when the time came, I used it to teach Ashley to drive. I'm not sure either Momma or Daddy ever drove with Ashley to evaluate her abilities. They outsourced the task to me. This sits uncomfortably in my soul, a gigantic lump of guilt and anxiety and blame. I was the one who mostly taught Ashley to drive, and Ashley died driving.

It happened in the summer before her senior year. On the day of her accident, August 12, she'd begged Momma to let her take the Tempo to the lake with her friends. She'd been allowed to drive to the lake the day before and nothing had gone wrong, so Momma acquiesced to this second solo trip. Ashley came into the den and asked if I wanted to go, too, but I said no. I was working a summer job at Subway, saving money to go to Bryn Mawr, which would start exactly two weeks later. This was one of my days off, and I just wanted to sit in my pajamas and watch *Lonely Planet* and another favorite travel show.

At about two in the afternoon, Momma got worried because Ashley was out past her curfew. She needed to go to the store, so she took Courtney and went out in the minivan to look for Ashley and run errands, bringing the gigantic, clunky car phone Daddy kept in his plumbing truck. So I was home alone when the county sheriff drove up with the First Baptist minister.

What I know about that day is this: Ashley took a curve too fast and hit gravel on the side of the road. The Tempo fishtailed out of control. It went into a field where it hit a fire hydrant. If it had just hit the hydrant, that might have been okay, but apparently lots of people had been hitting the hydrant on that curve, so the county had erected a concrete post in front of it to protect it. The Tempo hit the post and flipped. If Ashley hadn't been buckled up, she might have been thrown from the car, but she was buckled. Her window was open, and her head hung out of it and hit the post as the car flipped. She died immediately.

One of her friends was with her in the car and broke a leg in several places. Two other friends were behind her in another car, and when they pulled up, they passed out at the sight. For some reason, her Scooby-Doo backpack was in the back seat of the car, labeled with the classes she was preparing to take that fall. That detail still breaks my heart every time I visualize it.

When the sheriff and the minister pulled up to the house, I went out to see what was wrong. But they wouldn't tell me and asked me to get my mom home: that's when I knew something bad had happened to Ashley. I called Momma on the car phone. She said, "Ashley's dead, isn't she. I knew it!" And I said, "Momma, please just come home." I didn't want to tell her I suspected she was right: I didn't know why else the sheriff and a minister would be in our driveway. They stayed outside, and I went to my room and sat on the floor. When Momma pulled up, she grabbed her hair and came into the house screaming. Daddy was golfing, and people had to find him on the golf course: he arrived, drunk and confused, and started sobbing.

News travels fast in small towns, and people still had police scanners then. For a brief time, no one was sure whether it was me or Ashley—Courtney was only thirteen, so no one thought it was her—because it was my car, and the undertaker who saw her body, who went to our church, hadn't seen either of us in a while.

People flooded into the house immediately. I stayed in my room for a long time, then ambled through the rooms, disoriented, oddly embarrassed to be in my pajamas still, nodding vacantly at people. A car pulled up in our driveway. Darci climbed out of the passenger seat, her face white and grimly set, and marched purposefully toward the house.

I hadn't seen her in nearly three months, since I had graduated and she had not. She was really skinny. I came out to meet her on the porch, and as soon as she looked at me, I burst into tears. And then we were both sobbing, and we stood and hugged for a long time.

• • •

Teenagers died from car accidents regularly in Clinton, almost once a year. With every death, the town stopped, convulsed in a ritual of collective mourning. The school administration would pull us into a gym for an assembly to honor the life of the lost friend and to offer support and prayers for the grieving. It occurred to me later that no one ever questioned why they were dying, questioned the wisdom of letting kids drive at such young ages, unsupervised on curvy mountain roads, or wondered if they were drinking and driving and what that meant for the town. No one questioned how the town was taking care of its children or what the constant onslaught of grief might do to the ones who survived.

Kiaura Balentine noticed, as I had once, that this mourning ritual happened only with some children. Early in her senior year the town had come together to celebrate the life of a child who'd died from cancer and whose health struggle had been long and public and the subject of many people's prayers and fundraising efforts. Everyone wore red on a day the county judge proclaimed an official celebration of his life. Kiaura thought his life and his struggle had been inspiring, and she mourned his death. But she also noticed that no one had ever mentioned two of her classmates who had died during high school—a girl who committed suicide and a boy who drowned. She made a point to note their passing in her valedictory speech and wondered whether it was only kids from the "right" families who went to the "right" churches whose deaths became town events.

When I was a sophomore, a football player died in a car accident. He'd fallen asleep at the wheel. Everyone missed school the day of his service, except for us. Momma didn't like funerals in general, and we didn't go to many family funerals because she thought it was maudlin to have children grieving publicly. She couldn't easily stand the wailing and loud sobbing and Jesus talk that accompanied country funerals. When she didn't allow us to go to the football player's funeral, one of Ashley's friends asked her, "Come on, Ashley, where's your school spirit?" I thought it was gross, and though his death was tragic, I thought too many students were using it as an excuse to miss school.

In the immediate aftermath of Ashley's death, our house was full of friends and acquaintances and people we didn't know. They brought a constant supply of Mexican chicken casseroles and green beans and chicken and dumplings and other things we wouldn't eat. My bosses at Subway sent a giant plate of sandwiches.

The people who came and went talked a lot about God in ways that made my mom uncomfortable. *God's will is mysterious. God is taking care of Ashley now. When God wants to call you home, there's nothing you can do.* It was a practiced acceptance of death, no matter the circumstances. "Kathy, I really believe, if Ashley had been sitting right next to you that day, she would have dropped dead," someone we know—I can't remember who—had told my mom. She meant that Ashley had died because it was her predestined time, and even if she hadn't crashed the car that day, she would have met her end regardless. Momma thought, but didn't say, *I bet you do really believe that.* These well-meaning people were trying to circumvent our mourning. How could you be sad if someone you love went to heaven? And I felt pressure to rejoice in death, to see it as a new beginning, the true beginning after our exile on earth. It was a stark demonstration of the limits people in Clinton set on control over their own lives.

I felt a lot of things after Ashley died, but mostly uncontrollable rage. I hated that my extraordinary, resilient sister had died in such an ordinary way. I hated every mourner for coming to visit, for coming to her funeral, and that was a lot of people to hate, because it turned out that Ashley was one of the people whose passing the town wanted to mark. She would be the student in the memorials that school year, and there might be a gym assembly for her, and a page in our yearbook would be dedicated to her memory. I hated it all.

And I hated how quickly her story was rewritten. "Oh, Ashley was so funny!" people would say to us. "She was such a good actress!" But I remembered well how mean they'd been to her when she was alive. When she couldn't quiet her Tourette syndrome or her obsessive impulses, they'd disapproved. When she couldn't stop acting out after the joke was over for them but not for her and her uncontrollable body, they'd been annoyed. When she wore her curtain-like pants, they'd thought she was weird. She'd been so unhappy, and she'd so wanted to get out of Clinton. Now she never would. She became less complicated in death, and Clinton had an easier time loving her for it.

A week after Ashley died, the minister at the Methodist church, who had been the most supportive of me going to Bryn Mawr, came over, worried that I might not go after all. "Oh yes," I said. "I'm still going." Maybe if I had come from a different family, or from a different place, I would have taken a semester off or delayed my start. But my acceptance felt too tenuous, too thin a thread connecting me to everything I wanted my future to hold, and I feared losing it if I didn't leave immediately. Just before Ashley died, I'd gotten a packet in the mail, listing my roommates and my dorm room number and the addresses of my new fellow students from all over the country. Ashley had pored over the papers, even memorizing the names of my new classmates. At her funeral, one of her pallbearers, a coach she was close to, hugged me and said, "Do good in school."

There was no way I wasn't going. I was going to leave this stupid town and its stupid rocky soil where nothing grew and where children were buried; its stupid churches and hypocritical Holy Rollers; its stupid schools and the principal who, I thought, had kicked my best friend out of school; its poverty and its poverty of imagination; its low expectations; its girls who were expected to wear makeup and curl their hair and marry so young and produce an endless supply of babies; its stupid selective mourning, this stupid town that cared more about people who died than those who lived and struggled and couldn't find their way.

Less than two weeks after we buried Ashley, my mom, my dad, Courtney, and I piled into the minivan and began our long, mostly silent drive halfway across the country. "Ashley was supposed to hang out with me until I made friends" was all I remember Courtney, a high school freshman, saying.

We were determined to get past Tennessee the first day, a long, boring state, all on the same, ceaseless monotony of Interstate 40. We passed Nashville, where I would have stopped if I'd gone to Vanderbilt, and that was the farthest east I'd been in a car. We passed far out of Clinton's orbit, far out of my imagined universe, far past the places people had expected me to go to college. We passed through the state of Virginia and the next day we passed into Pennsylvania and out of the South. We passed through Amish country, where my dad bought a funny T-shirt in Intercourse, Pennsylvania, and I realized that this was only the third family vacation that I could remember taking. We passed into suburban

Philadelphia and went to a gigantic mall, where I bought a new pair of jeans from Banana Republic—the most I'd ever spent on a single item of clothing—to wear on my first day of orientation. We passed through the Gothic arches that framed Bryn Mawr's campus, the first time I'd ever seen it in person, and we walked into my room and met my roommates.

The summer after my freshman year, I did go back to Clinton, to work at Subway again and save money. Everyone there looked at me like I was a ghost. Meanwhile my Bryn Mawr classmates certainly weren't spending their summers working in fast-food restaurants, and for the rest of my college years, I found ways to stay and work in the Philadelphia area that also built up my résumé. After I graduated and moved to New York, I went home less and less often, even missing the holidays, until some years I did not go home at all.

My mom had sacrificed a measure of her own happiness to get me out of Clinton, and in leaving, I realized her dream and mine. But I sacrificed something too. When I left the town behind, I lost its people. Darci stayed in touch for a while. She wrote me long letters and told me she was going to be an extra in a movie directed by Billy Bob Thornton, who was from Arkansas and had just become a big star with the indie hit *Sling Blade*. She told me how Ashley had influenced her and how she wanted to pursue creativity and music because Ashley had been so talented. She thought her own creativity had been nurtured in our house and by our friendship. She had visited my mom in the days after Ashley's death.

I don't remember responding to her, though I wish I had. In that raw time, I found the depth of Darci's mourning confusing, and I closely guarded my own grief. I was away from home and my family, but I wanted to feel that anguish over Ashley was mine alone. She was my sister. She belonged to me.

I could have continued to be friends with Darci, or with anyone from Clinton, but I didn't want to, or really, I thought I couldn't. They were what I sacrificed. I excised them all from my life and went forward in college as if I had no history. After a while I avoided even Ashley's memory. It is hard to tell people that you had a sister who died. Everyone knows you have a mom and a dad, even if they don't know them, but siblings are less predictable. I would have had to introduce her existence and in the same breath say she was dead. Eventually, I solved it with an easy answer: I had one sister. Courtney was my only sister. I had lost no one. I had no one that I mourned, no one that I missed. I needed to constantly move into the future, I thought, to keep from being pulled back.

When I did reconnect with Darci many years later, she said she'd often wondered if I was mad at her for staying in Clinton, and for not doing the things we said we were going to do. When she said that, I realized I had been, unconsciously. I was angry with her for leaving me, for making me go out into the world alone. The anger sat there, buried with all of the guilt and grief and sadness and rage and hate surrounding Ashley's death, all thrumming at the same low frequency, somewhere deep in my psyche. But of course, I was the one who'd done the leaving.

Part II

Effects

10.

Leaving and Staying

My mom's mother died in the February of my last semester of college. Grandma had been living alone in the cabin Grandpa built on the Farm since he'd died at sixty-five from a heart attack shortly after retiring thirteen years before. Some of the land the cabin sat on went to my uncle, but he and Momma and her two living siblings, a brother and a sister, put the rest of it in a family trust as a way to honor their dad. In the years that followed, one sibling squabble after another broke the trust apart. Within ten years, the portion of the land they'd meant to preserve lay overgrown and unused, the cabin my grandparents had built was falling down, and the roses Grandma had tended so carefully were dying in a tangled mess. This land, which had been in his family since at least 1920, had meant so much to Grandpa that he'd returned from California to buy it, so much that we'd poured dirt from his hayfield over his coffin. But my mom and her siblings couldn't agree on what to do with their weighty legacy, so they did nothing. Something similar was happening to my hometown: old houses crumbling back into the earth, farms were given over to sedge grasses and reforestation or, worse, were clear-cut for timber. Properties had been left in trusts, like ours, to grandchildren and great-grandchildren who lived far away or didn't care enough to reconcile the state of their inheritances. They all belonged to people who for some reason were unable to offload them, or maybe unable to let them go.

Like many displaced Southerners, I developed a complicated relationship to the place where I'd grown up. I couldn't maintain the fury I'd felt when I'd moved away. Time, distance, and nostalgia did their work until it was burned out. I mourned that I hadn't always appreciated the better parts of country life: the beauty of my grandparents' farm, the taste of pepper vinegar on turnip greens, a canoe ride down a river fat with spring rains, a quilt raffle to benefit the local library, the easy fun of a county fair on a muddy autumn night, the slow and considered rhythms.

As I got older, Momma often talked about these things appreciatively. She told me about quilting with Daddy when they were a newly married couple, and I tried to imagine his calloused hands holding a needle. Her linen closet was full of the blankets they'd made, inexpert but personal, and the throws Momma had crocheted. She talked about making jams when she was a kid, growing and pickling cabbages with Grandma. She told me Daddy had sung in impromptu bluegrass bands, drunkenly and not very well, at the local VFW. Why hadn't I heard these stories sooner? Why hadn't she taught Courtney and me quilting and cooking while we were growing up? Why hadn't we spent more time helping Grandma tend her roses? We might have appreciated these things better if we had. It didn't occur to me until later that my mom's anger, like mine, came from trying to love a place that always disappointed her in the end.

I especially came to regret not keeping in touch with Darci. As my regret grew, it got harder to think about getting back in touch. So when she found me on Facebook in April 2015, just when I happened to be home, it felt like serendipity. For the rest of my two-week visit, I saw her almost every day. I went to her mom's house, and we sat at the kitchen table, chatting. We went to lunch together and walked through the courthouse square, as we'd done as children and teenagers.

The town had changed. Half of the courthouse square storefronts were empty, and many of the rest were run-down. Bill's Dollar Store, Burnett's five-and-dime, and Herschel's Texaco gas station were long gone. The furniture store had closed, and its building, which spanned nearly a full block and had beautiful native stone siding, stood empty, its windows bare but for a few old couches and tables that looked as though they'd been left behind after a clearance sale. The Ozark Café, where my mom had worked, was closed, and its building was dilapidated, with boarded-up windows. Most of the restaurants that remained were fast-food chains along the highway, which bypassed downtown. A few people walked back and forth between the courthouse and the handful of offices on the square—and the courtrooms were filled with defendants—but the eeriness of downtown overpowered any nostalgia I might have had.

Darci and I sat and talked about what had happened in the years after I'd left. Hearing about her life gave me a belated, achy homesickness I couldn't quite soothe.

After high school, she told me, she'd maintained her scholarships to the University of Central Arkansas in Conway. She got her GED, which was accepted in lieu of a diploma, and planned to enroll there in the fall of 1998. But when the time came, she switched to a small technical college in Little Rock, taking her state scholarships with her, because it had lower tuition. She moved to Conway with an older friend and planned to commute the thirty minutes to Little Rock. Because her state scholarships and her federal grants for low-income students amounted to more than the cost of tuition, she received a check for the surplus, about $1,500, as a stipend. She lived on that and partied in Conway, where she'd also gotten a part-time job at a pharmacy. But the half-hour commute from Conway to Little Rock, especially for early-morning classes, proved brutal, and the classes were boring. After only a week, she withdrew from college.

Darci soon spent all her remaining scholarship money. She visited friends in Florida for a while, but by early 1999 she was back home in Virginia's house. She stopped in on my mom once, covered in tattoos, Momma told me afterward, remarking that all the ink must weigh more than Darci herself because she was so skinny. Darci had prattled on about how she was going to be a musician or an actress, all because of Ashley. It was a weird visit, Momma told me, and if there was warning in her voice, I didn't hear it. By then I'd stopped talking much to anyone from home and was busy in college, happy to be far away.

When Darci and I met up again in the spring of 2015, she was still living with Virginia and her stepdad, David, this time in a rental about a mile from my mom's. She had two children. The house where they all lived was odd. The door from the carport opened into the kitchen, which featured an old, farmhouse-style wooden kitchen table. Next to the kitchen was a living room, with worn shag carpet, and a second living room, where furniture and boxes and old desks and unused computers and bookshelves lined all the wall space. The window shades looked as if they had never been opened. Darci's kids were jammed into two small bedrooms at the end of a short hall; off to the side, at the rear of the house, was the master bedroom, where Virginia and David slept. Darci slept on the couch in the second living room. Weekly lunch menus from school hung from pins on the wall, along with notes about doctors' appointments. Virginia, at sixty-two, would come home from work and head straight to the kitchen to cook supper for Darci and the kids, just as she had when we were in school. I imagined Virginia was tired of cooking suppers. The house felt dark and claustrophobic.

Darci kept piles of photo albums and scrapbooks from child-hood and maintained them well, in a way that was touching and old-fashioned. After an adulthood of moving from one apart-ment to the next, and shifting my life mostly online, I didn't have anything like that. She and I spent a couple of afternoons going through her albums. There were pages full of pictures of Ashley and me and our other friends. There were articles from our dance performances and state fair victories and Darci's years as a starter in basketball. There were also clippings of her school honors—from the year she won the county spelling bee in middle school and the year we were on a team for a problem-solving competition called Odyssey of the Mind. She kept a clip of the announcement that she'd gotten a scholarship to UCA, which noted she planned to major in psychology.

The highlights of the scrapbook, though, were the clippings about the band she'd formed when she moved back to Clinton, called Darci Daze. While I was in college, she was traveling the region performing at small music festivals with names like June Jam, in old fields, in mountains, in folk centers, and in parks. She never talked about being a musician while we were in school, but her mom's family had always been talented, and now Darci was hoping to build a career in music. Virginia played both the piano and the organ for her Seventh-day Adventist congregation, and the other members of her family joined choirs and played guitars and sang in old tent revivals. Darci's interest in music led to a rift with her friend Kasey, who had ditched school with her, left Kan-sas State University before her first semester ended, and was back in town. Over the next decade Kasey would earn a modest living playing in rock and country bands in bars and clubs in Fayetteville and Hot Springs, and she'd win a statewide performing contest modeled on *American Idol*. She thought Darci's interest in music was just a whim, and after a mutual friend hired Darci instead of

Kasey to play at her wedding, they fought and never made up. Losing Kasey isolated Darci and further disconnected her from who she had been in high school.

In the pictures of Darci performing, she's thin and tattooed, as Momma described her. Her hair is piled atop her head, a little curly. She wears halter tops, keeping her midriff bare, and long skirts or cargo pants. Her band played folk, 1960s rock, and anything else that suited them at the moment. "I was really getting into my music," she told me. "I was writing songs, I was playing in a band. It was probably not going anywhere, but I was learning and living part of my dream." She'd never really had a firm grasp on what she wanted to be when she grew up, she told me, interested in everything but easily distracted by the next new thing. Music was different, she said—maybe remembering it more fondly than was merited, but it clearly was important for her then.

Darci performed at the first Archey Fest, a country music festival, in 1999. She kept a copy of the front-page newspaper article, with a big picture of her holding a microphone and the band behind her.

"Isn't that cool?" Darci said. "We had people screaming, 'Encore! Encore!' for us." Her band came back out and performed the Janis Joplin song "Me and Bobby McGee."

She told me about her stint as an extra for the Billy Bob Thornton movie that she'd mentioned in her letter. She'd been sitting outside on the sidewalk to smoke a cigarette when Thornton came out of his trailer. All day the extras had been annoying the stars by asking for autographs, so she decided to give him a break. "I'm not going to ask you for your autograph," she said to him, "but will you do me one favor? Because I don't know what's going to happen in the years to come. Will you just remember my name?" She went on: "It didn't seem to shock him or anything. For the rest of the day, anytime he saw me, he would point and go, 'Darci Brawner, Darci Brawner, Darci Brawner.' It was so cool."

Darci would still have been young and hopeful then, still plan-
ning to astound the world, still believing she could get in a car and
drive anywhere and do anything. Maybe she could have. She could
have moved to a more creative city and found an outlet for her
energetic spirit. Darci told me she assumed she would leave Clinton but never got around to doing it. She never planned to stay.
She never really planned anything. Having a future elsewhere was
always a half-formed idea in the back of her mind.

Darci was so happy telling me these stories. On the spring afternoons we were together, we sat in a park filled with high school
students after school let out—cheerleaders practicing, getting
ready for summer camp; softball teams meeting for practices. She
flipped through the album pages quickly, remembering that time
of youth and adventure, laughing, her eyes bright, her laugh easy.
I tried not to let her see my own sadness for her, which I would feel
a lot as we got to know each other again. She was remembering a
moment when she had held such hope for a future, but all I could
think was that her dreams had ended then too.

• • •

On my first day at Bryn Mawr, after my parents, Courtney, and I
moved my boxes and suitcases into my room, we went walking
around campus. The day was almost unbearably bright. It was the
two-week anniversary of Ashley's death, and a panicky kind of
sorrow followed us. I thought I would fall apart if I had to continue smiling and introducing myself to people. We were looking
for my dean, who had sent me a letter to welcome me to the school
and whose name was one of the few I knew.

Not far from my dorm, we approached a tall building of concrete and rock, with slim windows and a massive staircase, looking official enough that administrators might lurk inside, but the

glass doors were locked. The building turned out to be the library. Someone inside came out to ask if we needed help. I told her I needed to speak to my dean, but I did not know where to find her. I don't remember whether I was crying or just on the verge.

"Don't worry," the librarian said, pointing across the green to a smaller building with a clock tower and patting me on the shoulder. "Bryn Mawr is a hard school to get into, but once you're here, they don't like to let you leave."

With her help, we found my dean. A family friend had sent her a letter detailing Ashley's death, and she'd just been reading it when we knocked on her door. She called the college's health center and arranged for us all to meet with a therapist there. I knew immediately I was in the right place.

The other students I met in the coming days reinforced this feeling. They liked the same movies and musicals that Ashley and I had treasured. One of my roommates hung a *Breakfast at Tiffany's* poster in our common room—one of our favorites. My college friends got my jokes, and I got theirs. It was the kind of place, I thought, that both Ashley and Darci would have liked.

• • •

My experience, leaving my depressed hometown to go to college, wasn't just my own personal experience. It was, in some ways, our national education policy, which emphasizes college as a way out of poverty. And it assumes that after college, students will move to wherever they can make the most money.[*]

---

[*] Since the 1980s and '90s, college graduates have earned ever higher wages, while the wages of high school graduates have remained stagnant, and wages for dropouts have fallen. This pattern varies to some extent by place. New York offers the highest of what economists call the "wage premium" for college graduates—they earn double what those with only a high school diploma bring

The result is a rural brain drain, as it's often called, but it's really a drain of people, resources, and opportunities. In 2009 sociologists Maria Kefalas from St. Joseph's University in Philadelphia and Patrick Carr from Rutgers University published an ethnography of a small town in Iowa, which they gave the pseudonym Ellis, called *Hollowing Out the Middle: The Rural Brain Drain and What It Means for America*. They had spent the summer of 2001 in Ellis, studying the lives of high school graduates: Which of them left town, and why?

I was more interested in the other side: Which students stayed, or left but returned home quickly, and why? Many Ellis graduates, the sociologists found, who forayed out of town found themselves unprepared for the world. Some did not like living in areas with higher populations of Black Americans—just as some people in Clinton don't like Little Rock because of its racial diversity. They were unprepared, or unwilling, to mingle with people who didn't look like them or who had different belief systems and backgrounds.

These students' distaste for cities confirmed for them that their hometowns were safer than the big, seemingly dangerous world. It's no surprise, then, that the people who stay in, or return to, small hometowns tend to be more conservative, both politically and socially. A 2016 survey from the Public Religion Research Institute and *The Atlantic* found that 57 percent of white adults who lived in their hometowns preferred Donald Trump in that year's presidential election, compared with 40 percent of those

---

in, while in Wyoming college graduates earn only 20 percent more, according to a 2020 report from the Thomas B. Fordham Institute. Arkansas is in the middle, at almost 70 percent. As the wage gap between college graduates and everyone else has continued to expand, the country's focus, since No Child Left Behind went into effect in 2002, has been on pushing everyone toward more education.

who lived farther than a two-hour drive from where they'd grown up. This points to a feedback loop for the insular, small-town dynamic: the people who think their small towns are the best often haven't lived far away for a significant period of time and so don't have a solid basis for comparison.

Those who never left Ellis tended to have more working-class and low-income backgrounds. These class systems are reproduced in high school: the students with good grades from middle- and upper-income families were nurtured and encouraged by adults to go on to college, while the students from lower-income families didn't have such expectations placed upon them. One student at the high school in Ellis, struggling with his studies, was encouraged to leave school to "quit wasting everyone's time." It reminded me of my friend April's observation that Clinton High School teachers invested more in the students who were bound for college than in those likely to stay in their hometown. So those who stayed were less likely to have their talents nurtured and their futures planned or supported. These students often came from backgrounds of financial struggle, and their futures promised more of the same, more limited growth and opportunities. Small towns like Clinton offered them few good job prospects and not much to do. In another era, such young people might have worked on the family farm or small business and ultimately taken it over, but most of those small-scale enterprises have gone by the wayside. The young people I spoke to in high school took it for granted that they would have to move away to find jobs, whether they wanted to or not. And when high school graduates move away, rural hometowns experience continued population loss.

Another feedback loop at work in these depopulated counties is the loss of essential services. In western Van Buren County, which is very rural, two school systems closed in the 2000s when enrollment fell below a number newly mandated by the state.[*] The U.S. Postal Service began closing rural post offices in 2012. These losses caused property values to plummet and pushed people in these counties to leave. In many official ways, parts of rural America no longer exist.

People who returned to Clinton with degrees[†] often filled the same roles their parents had: they were dentists, doctors, lawyers, business owners, and teachers. They went to the same churches they'd grown up in and lived much as they had growing up. A few of them returned with the idea that they would improve people's lives here, but most came back because they liked Clinton and because their families had been successful here and still lived here. Few thought anything in town needed to change, so nothing much ever did. They thought of themselves as town leaders, and they were well enough off to weather any storms Clinton suffered. But this small group of town elite were the exceptions: most of the people who stayed in town were the worst off, with the least prospects.

When the majority of high school graduates don't start their adult lives in their rural birthplaces, they don't buy homes there, get married, have children, and enroll them in their alma maters. They don't start jobs and businesses, volunteer, or bring back the expertise they've acquired elsewhere. The result is a smaller property tax base, fewer kids in schools, fewer jobs, and other signs of decline. Fewer people come in with new ideas and new money and earning power—the dynamism that drives city life. These towns are less likely to have robust civic institutions or services to help people. All these factors affect health, well-being, and life expec-

---

[*] In Arkansas, school districts must consolidate if their enrollment drops below 350 for K–12 for two consecutive years.
[†] In Van Buren County, only 15.8 percent of residents have at least a bachelor's degree.

tancy. Those with fewer years of education are much more likely to come from and continue to live in these disadvantaged communities. Measuring someone's level of education is, in some ways, a good indicator of where they might have grown up and what kinds of communities they live in now.

No wonder Darci lost momentum. In the years when she was trying to be a musician in Clinton, she wouldn't have found much support or mentorship or visibility, especially before Instagram and TikTok, YouTube, or even MySpace. Having a career in music was difficult even in cities with many resources: in a small town like Clinton, it was nearly impossible. Unable to make enough money from music to get out, and lacking a college degree, she was consigned to low-wage jobs. Clinton, like many small towns in rural America, was the kind of town you could get stuck in.

11.

The Party House

A few months after I met up with Darci again, I reconnected with another Clinton friend, Cassandra Ticer. At five foot eleven, broad and muscular, Cassandra is now a nurse and a long-distance runner who lives in an artsy neighborhood in North Little Rock, across the river from the capital city. Her skin is naturally tanned and freckled, her hair is light brown, and so are her eyes. Cassandra's an only child, and her mom had her at the age of sixteen. Most of her mom's family—three sisters and a brother—still live near each other on the mountains outside Clinton, supporting each other and their children and their children's children as one big, close-knit family. Cassandra is the outlier, and she doesn't visit often, which is a sore spot with her mom.

In high school, Cassandra dated an older boy she thought she'd marry. They'd have a couple of kids and live in a trailer near her mom. Or maybe they wouldn't marry, but she'd still have a couple of kids with him and put up a trailer near her mom. Instead, Cassandra's boyfriend broke up with her. She was devastated and took caffeine pills to lose weight, thinking that would tempt him back. She felt directionless without that future to look forward to. Then one of our teachers saw her in the hallway and confronted her: "Cassandra, how did you get so skinny? You're too smart to be on drugs!" Embarrassed, she stopped taking pills.

Her mom's only goal for her, Cassandra told me, was to graduate high school without getting pregnant. She achieved that
goal easily, but after that she didn't know what to do. Early in
our senior year, she had applied, somewhat absent-mindedly, to
Arkansas State University, in Jonesboro. Cassandra was an honors student and had higher-than-average scores on her college
admission tests, so she received a full scholarship covering tuition, room, and board. Without her boyfriend to keep her at
home, she decided to enroll. She did well for her first two years
of college, but then she decided to transfer to Henderson State
University and live off campus in a house with a bunch of guy
friends from high school. It was a decision she made without
parental or professorial input. She wanted to party more often
with her friends, so she did. Cassandra said it was one of the
defining moments of her life. "If I could go back and find
eighteen-to-twenty-one-year-old Cassandra, I would kick her
ass," she said.

Her grades plummeted, and she stopped going to class. "I was
home with my tail between my legs by Thanksgiving break. Did
not even withdraw from that semester. I have an entire semester at
Henderson that's just F's."

I knew many who went to college and struggled to stay. Some
dropped out immediately like Darci, while others, like Cassandra,
left after a few successful semesters even if they had full scholarships. They struggled to balance their studies with working at
jobs for spending money, car payments, and other expenses. Some
lost their scholarships after a semester or two because they
couldn't keep their grades high enough.

Many were prepared academically, leaving high school even as
honors students, as Cassandra had. But the required introductory
classes felt like repeats of high school classes and bored them.

Why should they pay to take subjects they'd already mastered?[*] Arkansas has strict requirements for the first two years of university education, and because Clinton didn't offer Advanced Placement classes at the time, students had no opportunities to bypass them. Peers of mine from Arkansas called these courses "the basics" and said that they were a boring grind.

Low-income students are more likely to enroll in the nearest state school or community college, but these schools may lack the resources to help students deal with unexpected problems and navigate complex institutions, or to provide challenging courses that will keep students enrolled.[†] Administrators largely leave them to navigate the byzantine systems of financial aid and credits and qualifications on their own. Darci's high school boyfriend Robin had dropped out of UCA because he was partying, and when he worried that he'd lost all his scholarships and financial aid, he hid from administrators rather than reach out to them for help.

Life at state schools couldn't have been more different from my experience at Bryn Mawr, where I was surrounded by an academic and mental health support system. My classes were interesting, I had few requirements to worry about, and when I needed help, I felt I could seek support from my professors or the dean. I had access to free counseling at the campus mental health center. I was

[*] Andrew Hacker, in *The Math Myth: And Other Stem Delusions* (2016), argues that the widespread requirement of Algebra II drives dropout rates both in high school and in college and should be replaced with a statistics course.
[†] In *Paying for the Party* (2013), sociologists Elizabeth A. Armstrong and Laura T. Hamilton detailed how many big state schools, even those with good academic reputations, cater to the needs of wealthier, paying students, whether high-achieving or not, rather than help low-income students stay enrolled. Additionally, many low-income students have parents who didn't go to college and lack the resources or knowledge to help them weather challenges.

able to work part-time and pay my small share of the tuition—around $200 every month of the school year—and still have enough left over for clothes and pizza with my friends on the weekends. (It wasn't enough to keep me out of debt, but that was a problem for later.) Even if I hadn't been hell-bent on staying away from Clinton, I would never have left this warm, supportive environment before graduating.

Back home, Cassandra pieced together three part-time jobs to make enough money to drive to classes at UCA, trying to stay on track. After a brief time back at her mom's house on the Mountain, she realized she needed a place closer to town. She rented an old farmhouse, owned by the mom of a friend of ours, and looked for roommates to share expenses with. That was when she found Darci.

• • •

When Cassandra asked Darci to room with her at the farmhouse, Darci jumped at the opportunity. Along with three other roommates, they split the monthly rent five ways. Darci went to work at a country club's restaurant near the resort town of Fairfield Bay. "She was driving a long way to this restaurant, but at the time it seemed like a lot of money," Cassandra told me. "She would make like a hundred dollars a shift. So she had a lot more disposable income than any of us."

Cassandra liked to drink on weekends, but the partying she saw at their house was more than she'd expected. Unencumbered by school or parents, Darci partied every night and took Soma pills recreationally. At one party, Cassandra remembered, Darci took so many pills that she fell to the floor and had to be carried up to her room, limp and unresponsive.

"It was so long ago and I kind of blocked it out," Cassandra told me. But one time Darci "had driven to work really, really messed up and . . . I think she fell asleep in her car when she got there and a co-worker had to drive her home. I think maybe that job ended after that."

Darci and Robin's friend Dan also remembered endless partying in Clinton. After dropping out of college, he returned home and strung together manual labor jobs. Without enough to engage him at work and not much to do for entertainment, he smoked weed, got drunk, and hung out with friends, he told me. His life was slowing down, and he thought it was because expectations in Clinton were too simple, too similar for everyone. He felt crushed by a depressing sameness. In Clinton "you find your wife, you have some kids, and you go to the Chuckwagon Races"—an annual rodeo-like event—"or you go eat at the fish house on Friday night. You've hit the big-time if you have . . . a four-wheel-drive truck, you go deer hunting . . . your kids play Little League Baseball and you go to First Baptist Church." That was life in Clinton, from your twenties until you died, he thought. If it wasn't the life you wanted or could make yourself want, you could spin out of control very quickly in an effort to find mental stimulation or fun. "There's nothing to look forward to," he told me. When I was young, I'd felt the way Dan did, with an additional dimension: the enormous pressure to want those things and nothing else. Within three years, Dan moved out and re-enrolled in college.

Like Dan, Cassandra felt she had to get out before her life got bogged down in ways she couldn't escape. Women in particular, she thought, didn't so much decide to stay in Clinton as get stuck there. You could get stuck when your partying made it hard to keep a job or to find a new one. You could get stuck when you had kids, which sometimes came out of the indiscriminate partying. She saw it all the time, women getting pregnant and falling into

relationships without giving much thought to who they were having kids with.

Cassandra decided to leave again. She moved to Conway and
worked as a nanny for a single mom in exchange for room and
board. She didn't finish college then but moved to Little Rock to
bartend, then found her way to nursing school in her late twenties. Her career has been on an upward trajectory ever since, and
she earned a bachelor's degree at thirty-nine. "I think about my
life, and my friends and my boyfriend, and if I had stayed in Clinton, there's no way I would have had this life or been exposed to
the things I've been exposed to," she told me. "I remember being
torn between wanting to be part of the cool crowd and knowing
that I didn't belong here, this was not for me, this was temporary.
I felt like I was toeing that line several times. I think one of my
saving graces was I just had no desire to do drugs. Like, none. I
could very well be . . . stuck there with a couple of kids from a
couple of different guys."

• • •

Cassandra's stories about partying sounded to me like stories of
frustrated youth trying to have the fun everyone seemed to have at
that age. While I was at Bryn Mawr, I went to parties like any college student and drank too much. Different types of drugs, from
pot to heroin, were always around. It seemed a normal part of life
on campus, then in New York, where I moved right after graduating. On weekend nights, my friends and I barhopped late, went to
clubs, stumbled home in the wee hours, hooked up randomly.
Eventually, most of us grew out of it and stopped.

But when I was partying in my twenties, it was outside the
judgment of our religiously conservative town in that still-dry
county. The teetotalers watched the sinners and judged them.

Someone once refused to hire my dad for a job because they knew he was a drinker. "I ain't never been drunk on the job!" he'd told me, hurt and offended. It wasn't his activities on the job that bothered religious conservatives—they disapproved of him drinking at all. The members of the anti-liquor Baptist church who dominated the town didn't distinguish clearly between social drinkers and alcoholics, and a person who was known to be either could find it hard to get a job.

So people drank even casually in secret, at bonfire parties deep in the woods or on private property. In the late 1990s and early 2000s, newer and harder drugs like meth and opioids were introduced, and the places where people had once gathered only to drink and smoke pot became safe places to use hard-core stimulants.

With Cassandra gone, Darci spent more and more time at parties on the Mountain. There in 2001, on my dad's family land, she ran into George Bigelow, tall and broad, with dark features. George is the son of the woman her dad had left Virginia for when we were in high school. He's also one of my second cousins on my dad's side. His dad, Robert, had worked for Daddy's plumbing company occasionally, but never as a steady employee. (Daddy only ever had one real employee, Robert's brother, Paul.) I never really knew George, he's about six years older than me, and our paths didn't cross much in school. But he was part of the jumbled, confusing branch of my family that lived together on the Mountain. Darci knew him a little—they became step-siblings when her father married his mother—but after her parents' divorce, she avoided him and his family. At twenty-six, he had already been to prison for felony drug charges, breaking and entering, and theft. He had two sons with a woman closer to his age with whom he no longer had a relationship.

That night Darci was playing guitar, singing a Janis Joplin

song, when she saw George sitting at a bonfire. He smiled, and she felt good about him. *He has a good heart, and he's a good person*, she'd thought. But she was into the bad boy thing anyway. "And I still am," she'd tell me when we met up again. "And that's terrible. I'm like, if you have tattoos and you're on parole, you know," she said, and laughed.

Darci and George eventually hooked up. She told me they got along easily, and he treated her well in the beginning. He wasn't a sweet talker—mostly she hooked up with him because he was there. "It's so sad," she said, and laughed. "Why am I with any man?"

George's calculation about why they got together was simpler. "I had drugs," he told me when I interviewed him later. "She wanted drugs."

12.

Motherhood

Darci and George hung out frequently, finding each other at parties, talking about their connections. George admired my dad, she told me, and they talked about him and my family often. My dad had nicknamed him Pudge. George encouraged her to get back in touch with me—I was away at Bryn Mawr—but she never did. Their relationship was casual, almost accidentally romantic, and not exclusive at first, like a lot of relationships in our early twenties. I wouldn't have considered anyone I was dating a serious partner at that age. Darci said it was the same for her.

She was living at her mom's house, commuting to the two-year college in Morrilton. "It just wasn't interesting to me, the classes," she said. She never declared a major and didn't know what she wanted to do. "It was kind of a catch-22: I went to just get my basics, but I got bored with it because I didn't have a goal. . . . But I didn't have a goal because I didn't want to commit to something." Throughout, she stayed with George wherever he was on the Mountain at some relative's house, and in the spring of 2002, right before my college graduation, she found out she was pregnant. She was about to turn twenty-two.

This part of Darci's life is hard for me to imagine. At that age, I was on birth control, and she wasn't. Twice in my young adulthood, I went to the nearest Planned Parenthood clinic and took a morning-after pill, just in case, because a condom had broken or I'd had some similar scare. Darci didn't live near a clinic. Our lives were shaped by our behavior but also by the places where we lived. I and everyone I knew in college and my young adulthood took it for granted that we would plan our families once we accomplished our other goals. But where Darci lived, the default for women was to have children, whether they planned it or not.

Darci found out she was pregnant during a hospital visit, and it was as if a switch went off. *I'm pregnant. I'm going to just be a mother and just do this,* she thought. It was, in some ways, her first real goal. In 2005 the sociologists Kathryn Edin and Maria Kefalas (who also worked on the study of small-town Ellis, Iowa) wrote the seminal ethnology on low-income women and motherhood, *Promises I Can Keep: Why Poor Women Put Motherhood Before Marriage.* The women they interviewed didn't put off motherhood because they had no reason to, and even looked forward to motherhood as their first success. Edin and Kefalas's work challenged the notion that low-income women had children simply because they had unplanned pregnancies and lacked access to abortion or birth control. They found that often women chose to have children and pursued motherhood even when it meant they would struggle.

Darci wanted to become a mother. She hadn't graduated high school, wasn't likely to have a music career, and was struggling to stay in college, which she found boring and pointless. Being a mom would give her something to do. It helped that many women she knew in Arkansas, whether they had gone to college or not, became mothers in their early twenties.*

---

* In a 2018 analysis conducted for *The New York Times,* Caitlin Myers, a Middlebury College economist who studies reproductive health, found that the average age at which a woman in Arkansas has her first child is twenty-two, as opposed to twenty-six nationally. The high rate of teen births is pulling the

• • •

There's a lot of pressure for motherhood to be the only thing that matters to women. This message is often explicit. Mary Kassian, a Southern Baptist educator and writer, often laments the dominant "Girl Power" cultural messages that encourage women to earn degrees and get jobs outside the home. She fell for this earlier in her own life, she says, until she learned that to be a truly strong woman, she would need to be weak so she could submit herself to Christ. Katelyn Beaty, the editor of the largest evangelical publication, *Christianity Today,* has written about how she and most evangelical women long viewed motherhood as life's "central call" and struggled over whether working outside the home was sinful. In her 2016 book *A Woman's Place,* she argues against that notion, but in the evangelical world, as a rare full-throated advocate for women working, she is rare.

Women in Clinton spoke to me of pregnancy the way they did about everything else, as if it were something that alighted from the universe that they were powerless to prevent or end. "Before I formed you in the womb, I knew you," God says to Jeremiah, the weeping prophet whose life is beset with trials and tribulations. "Before you were born I set you apart; I appointed you as a prophet to the nations."

Where women must give themselves up to the unknowable and divine plans of God, there is no such thing as an unplanned pregnancy. Arkansas has one of the strongest anti-abortion popula-

---

state's average down. In general, over the past few generations, the average age at which women become mothers has been going up, but that trend is strongly influenced by education level. Women with more formal education tend to wait to have children, while those with less have children at younger ages, and their lives are often less secure. It's another inequality gap.

tions in the country.* Even as other parts of the country relaxed their attitudes on abortion and women's reproductive choices, in Arkansas the opposition became even stronger. Most of the women I knew growing up weren't even regularly on birth control. For women living in poverty, according to the Kaiser Family Foundation, tubal ligation is one of the most common methods of birth control. Women tend to have two or three children at relatively young ages, then once they've had all the children they can handle, they get their tubes tied in their late twenties or early thirties. This gap is replicated across America. Darci didn't feel as if she had an alternative to having her child with George.

All the messages, both subtle and overt, we'd absorbed as girls—abstinence-only education, the belief that girls are only future mothers subservient to men, the lack of opportunities for women's success in other realms—seemed to converge to make the decision for her.

It came at the moment when Darci felt she was supposed to become a grown-up, as several people said to me. She cleaned up her act and stopped using when she was pregnant. A friend of Ashley's who'd been with her the day she died told me she drank too much after the accident, sitting through the night and watching the sun set and rise again, thinking about her own death, and medicating her depression with alcohol, until she got pregnant with her first child. Motherhood was supposed to be a turning point, when women subsumed all their own worries for the sake of their children. When I asked Cassandra if she thought Darci had ever had an opportunity to do something different with her life, she said, "I would like to think that she had two chances with her children." Even Cassandra, the only other Clinton graduate I

---

* In the Pew Research Center's regular surveys on the issue, 60 percent of Arkansans say abortion should be illegal in all or most cases.

knew who'd remained childless, as I had, into her forties, sub-scribed to this magical thinking, to some degree. In Clinton, motherhood is supposed to be the force that corrects all past mis-deeds and gives women a new purpose. Darci thought having a child would grow her up.

Darci and George moved into a little rental house near her mom's on School Hill. These two people, plainly ill suited, had fallen in together to welcome a child into the world because that's what people did in Clinton. They let God decide their fates. Vir-ginia told me that Darci's being with George was the first time she thought Darci might be on the wrong track. Darci, bookish and artistic and still potentially headed back to college someday, was now tethered to a man who had a reputation for violence and a history of trouble. But she didn't intervene or counsel Darci to choose another direction. She shrugged and said, "If that's what she wants to do, I can't make her change her mind."

Aside from their child, Darci and George seemed to be together mainly because they found themselves in the same place. Cassan-dra pointed out that in Clinton, many women married or moved in with a man early, then divorced to marry someone else. They might do that a few times in a roller-coaster pattern of moving in and moving out and changing last names and changing identities. "I don't think there's a love at all," Cassandra said. "Because also, how can you find people in a town of two thousand?"

Darci's daughter, Maddie, was born in November 2002. I had just turned twenty-three and was living in New York, working at my first job after college, trying to figure out what I wanted to do with my life. Arkansas felt far away, and I rarely went home be-cause I didn't want to and didn't have the money or vacation days to fly back. When I saw people during my few trips home, it was almost always accidental: I bumped into them at Walmart or in town. I hoped to run into Darci that way, but I never did. It had been many years since I'd heard from her, as if she'd disappeared, and I hadn't yet reckoned with my own role in our neglected friendship. Occasionally, news of friends from high school getting married, having babies, and sometimes getting divorced trickled out to me, but it seemed to come from a different world. If I'd gotten pregnant at that point in my life, I would have unapologetically considered it a disaster. Not for many more years would my college and work friends get married and deliberately plan their families, so different from women in Arkansas.

After Darci's daughter was born, I learned she was with George and worried for her. I suspected that she wasn't doing well, that her partnership with George had been accidental and was not healthy, and that she'd stumbled into motherhood without necessarily being ready for it.

After we reconnected, Darci told me that having Maddie had given her life purpose and direction and that George was a good father. But she also said that while Maddie was a baby, she imagined leaving George and Clinton behind. She still had fantasies about going somewhere new and starting a new life with her daughter in tow. Just the two of them, Maddie and Darci against the world.

She didn't, though. She stayed in Clinton and stayed with George and had another child with him, a son, Kai, four years later, in 2006. By the time we were twenty-seven, when I took my first job as newspaper reporter, Darci was already mother to two young children whose father she had never married and wasn't sure she loved.

13.

The Money

The fortunes of rural towns like Clinton collapsed during my young adulthood, from 2000 to 2010. The period was marked by recessions—the dot-com bust, the economic slump after 9/11, and the Great Recession. But those disasters laid bare a longer-running problem, a contraction of good jobs and an expansion of low-paying ones in the service sector at places like Walmart, which began in Arkansas. On the East Coast, I entered job markets that were vibrant and growing, however fitfully, but in my hometown and places like it, the manual labor jobs once fueled by the building and infrastructure booms started to disappear.

Blue-collar families in 2018 were essentially making the same amount of money as their counterparts had in 1978, so even in the best circumstances, Darci and George might have brought in approximately what our parents had made thirty years before. The Great Recession, which began at the end of 2007, finally made the decline obvious. In rural places like Clinton, the bottom fell out of the economy, and people who'd forgone college to work their way up found that there was no up to get to.

In 2008 the chicken-processing plant next to the middle school, where my grandparents and Darci's dad had worked, closed. In 2006 a plant that had made electrical cords closed. In 2013 a frozen food company moved into that space, promising to hire hundreds; it hired about a dozen instead. In 2008 a boat factory that employed about eighty was hit by a massive tornado, and it did not survive.

The natural gas boom allowed people in Arkansas and in Pennsylvania, Oklahoma, North Dakota, and a few other states to stave off full-blown disaster. At first, people made money selling the mineral rights to their land, or from natural-gas production, and local men were hired to build the platforms for gas wells and to work in the industry. A handful of people around the county hit the lottery, earning millions. The boom was short-lived. The price of natural gas plummeted in 2009. There had been too much supply, and with the recession, the companies left for Texas, where the gas was easier and more profitable to extract. Jobs left with them. A few people stayed with the industry, commuting by plane for long workweeks, or traveling by RV to jobs and coming home to Arkansas in the off periods. But even those jobs had become scarce.

The Great Recession widened the gap between the most and least well-off areas of the United States in what the Brookings Institute called the Great Reshuffling. The places where the economy not only bounced back but thrived, where jobs grew and businesses were created, were concentrated on the coasts, especially the Northeast Corridor and the Pacific Northwest, and in a few places in between: Utah, Colorado, Minnesota, Wisconsin, and Texas. Suburban and urban zip codes did best. The most prosperous zip codes also had higher rates of educational attainment, with 45 percent of the country's advanced degree holders living in them. These trends persisted through the Covid-19 pandemic. Black Americans, Latinos, and rural whites, on the other hand, are more likely to live in "distressed" zip codes, places losing both jobs and people. A third of Arkansas's population lives in a distressed zip code. These places, where the least educated white Americans are clustered, are unlikely ever to recover.

The place that less-educated white people occupy in the national fabric has changed as well. Once farmer-settlers, they have now been left behind by progress. As Isabel Wilkerson writes in her 2020 book *Caste: The Origins of Our Discontents,* the United States is best understood as a society with a modern caste system, a rigid racial hierarchy created before our country's birth. While Blacks are at the bottom of the hierarchy, the least-educated whites are the lowest ranking among the dominant group. Even when people in this group knew they weren't the best off, what kept them from feeling that they were at the very bottom was the color of their skin.

Political scientists, Wilkerson writes, call white Americans' response to recent social changes "dominant group status threat." Consciously or not, they feel they are entitled to some measure of security and comfort based on their whiteness, to privileges that were afforded previous generations of their families, and they react with cultural fury and depression when that is threatened. They benefited from a system that relied on the oppression of people of color, especially Black Americans, but they resisted that truth. In her 2021 book *The Sum of Us,* Heather McGhee, a former president of Demos, a think tank that promotes racial and economic equality, writes that these two trends are of a piece: "Racial hierarchy offered white people a reprieve from the class hierarchy and gave white women an escape valve from gender oppression." Racism was used as a wedge to gain political support for policies, but when those policies ultimately drained public resources, they hurt many of the same white Americans who voted for them.

While the racial caste system hasn't gone away, an educational caste system has been laid alongside it, and people in areas like my home county *feel* they are losing status, even as the most highly educated Americans of any race move upward. "In the zero-sum stakes of a caste system upheld by perceived scarcity, if a lower-caste person goes up a rung, an upper-caste person goes down. The elevation of others amounts to a demotion of oneself, thus equality feels like a demotion," Wilkerson writes. ". . . Thus, a caste system makes a captive of everyone within it." This helps explain why many of those without college educations are so hostile to those who have one. Non-college-educated white Americans were the biggest voters for Donald Trump, and part of what they were rejecting was "elitism," an educational hierarchy that ranks them lowest. When Trump voters revolted, when they stormed the Capitol on January 6, 2021, part of what they wanted restored was a racial caste system that ranked them nearer the top because they were white: the Confederate battle flags they carried that day gave them away.

What the people of Clinton see all around them is decline and erosion, even as the rest of the country seems to be moving forward and somehow benefiting from what they've lost. Everything about the structure and culture of our town was unprepared for the new century. The lack of education, the lack of connections to good jobs, the departure of some young adults to pursue good work elsewhere all doomed those left behind after the recession.

• • •

When Darci became pregnant with Maddie, in 2002, George wanted her to quit playing music. She probably would have had to anyway: it never really paid her much, and she'd had to travel the state for days-long festivals. Camping out in the wilderness and taking a lot of drugs at late-night parties took their toll. Darci had always picked up jobs waitressing or in retail, but she didn't plan to as a mom. As was common in Clinton, her plan was to stay at home and raise Maddie, and later Kai, before they entered school.

In deciding not to work, Darci was tying herself to George, betting her good luck on his, waiving her chance at achieving independence and making more money down the road. One of the best jobs Darci had, as a carhop at Sonic, paid minimum wage plus tips, which was hardly worth the downsides of not being home to care for the kids, to cook and clean the house.

Women's decision not to work tends to keep them in poverty—they never quite fill the hole formed early in life. Moreover joblessness has long been linked with increased mortality. A 2013 study from the Harvard Center for Population and Development Studies tied the lowered life expectancy of the least educated white women in part to joblessness. Jobs provide intangible benefits besides money: independence, a social circle, a daily mission. They can curb harmful behaviors, like smoking all day.

Darci and George set out to live on what George made through the manual jobs he pieced together. He worked occasionally in a rock quarry south of town, near Bee Branch Mountain—rough, backbreaking work. He probably could have gotten a job with the Arkansas Highway Department, pouring hot asphalt onto rural highways, or with a local telephone company, climbing telephone poles. Early in his adulthood, he had hoped to become a plumber, like many men in his immediate family. He thought he could do the tough lifting and shoveling and moving those jobs required, as most young men I knew did. But those jobs became harder to get.

During their time together, Darci and George never lived above the poverty line. George worked sporadically, and Darci received support from government safety-net programs like food stamps; WIC, the food program for women, infants, and children; Medicaid; and housing vouchers. But they couldn't always pay rent, and they moved often, staying one step ahead of eviction. On one of my visits, Darci pointed out all the little rental houses she'd lived in, on School Hill and along the highway, never too far from town. In their first years together, she told me, she and George mostly partied on weekends but still showed up for their shifts and held down jobs. "It wasn't a party house," she told me, indicating one of their rental houses. But she took whatever pills she could get her hands on, while George moved to meth—even after the birth of their two children. She told me that during her pregnancies she'd used pot only for nausea, but I wasn't sure whether to believe that.

Despite all the obstacles of life in Clinton, some younger mothers thrived. Once their children were old enough to enter school, they went back to college or attended a training program and later built a career they enjoyed and became more stable. Usually, they had the support of their extended families, especially their moms, and they almost always jettisoned the man they'd made a bad match with early in their lives. They might settle down again later in more stable marriages. But for many reasons, Darci and George never married.*

The first seven years of Darci and George's life together—2001 to 2008—were especially hard. George was physically and emotionally abusive—he hit her, punched her, and was controlling—and the abuse escalated over time, she said. Their reputations as drinkers and partiers made it harder for them to be hired. Darci

---

* Marriage rates vary dramatically by educational attainment. A Pew Research Center analysis of Census Bureau data found that in 2015 (the last year data was available as of this writing), 65 percent of those with a college degree or higher got married, while only 50 percent of those with just a high school education did.

never asked her mom and stepdad for help, she told me, though she wondered later why she hadn't.

Maybe it was because Virginia and David had had legal custody of her brother Cody's son since he was an infant. Cody never did well in school and had been in and out of trouble since he was eighteen. In 2005 he was convicted of manufacturing and delivering a controlled substance and sentenced to five years probation. Cody's partner was equally unstable, so Virginia had stepped in to raise their son from the start. All the way back in elementary school, Darci had proudly brought home A's to soothe Virginia's worries about Cody. Virginia could easily become overwhelmed.

Maybe if Darci had turned to Virginia more for help in those early years, it would have curtailed some of the worse things that happened later, or maybe it would have made no difference at all.

When Maddie was three, they needed money, so Darci went back to work. In the winter of 2006, she found a job as a receptionist at Ferrellgas, a company that sold propane gas. She arrived to find the place a disorganized mess. Papers were strewn about on top of metal filing cabinets, cluttering everything. Few of the records had been transferred to a computer. The office smelled of printer ink and dust. She found uncashed checks for as much $200 in drawers and accounts that hadn't been updated for several payment cycles. She went in on weekends and worked overtime to update neglected accounts and organize the customer files.

Ferrellgas had a large tank in front of its retail store, where customers drove up in pickups and filled small containers with propane for gas grills and camping stoves. One day that spring an older man—neatly dressed in a polo shirt and khakis, his white hair parted down the side—came in to refill a small tank. Darci had had a bad day, fighting with George, and was too broke even to buy lunch. She and her family weren't starving, but she needed diapers and other household items, and she needed them before her next paycheck was due.

The man came over to her to pay for his tank. It came to thirty dollars, and he handed her cash. Darci started to fill out a receipt, but he said, "Oh, I don't need a receipt."

Initially she wondered, *Then where should I put a record of the money?* But an idea flashed through her brain in the next instant: with the absence of records, the misplaced payments, the fact that she was alone in the store . . . if she didn't write him a receipt, if she didn't write the transaction down, it would be like it had never existed. She thought, *Well, I'll just take it.*

Her thefts started out small like that, taking just extra grocery money here and there. But soon, when people came in to pay their monthly bills in cash, she pocketed ever larger sums. Once an older lady came in after church, wearing her Sunday dress, and paid her $200 bill with cash; Darci took it. People filled up their grill tanks throughout the summer; Darci took the proceeds. She even took some of the cash in the drawer and fiddled with the books to disguise what she'd done.

Darci gave birth to her son, Kai, that summer. She took two weeks off, then went back to work. Becoming a family of four escalated their problems with money. She continued to steal.

One day in early November 2006, Darci walked into the office to find nearly every boss, regional manager, and colleague she'd ever met going through the files—a half dozen people from around the state. One of them, a middle-aged man in a button-down shirt and glasses, introduced himself as a financial investigator for the company.

She thought, for a brief instant, about turning around and running away, but she couldn't do that. Instead, she sat down at the desk across from the investigator.

"We're coming up with all these weird spots in the balance sheets," he told her. "Deposits aren't matching up during the time frame that you've worked here." Then he asked straightforwardly: "Have you taken any of the money?"

In a panic, she answered, "Yeah, I took it."

He asked her for dollar amounts.

"There's no way I can know that. There was not any one time," she confessed in a blur. "Sometimes it was twenty dollars, sometimes it was a hundred dollars."

A woman from human resources sat down next to the investigator and nodded.

The investigator told Darci that Ferrellgas would do its own investigation, but someone from the county sheriff's office might too. "You're probably facing jail time, and possibly prison time for these charges," he said.

Darci had previously been in misdemeanor trouble for writing hot checks, but that now seemed minor in comparison. She was in serious trouble now. The investigator told her to leave, so she did. She'd known this day was coming, and in some ways, she was relieved that it was finally there. She sat in her car, an old Dodge minivan, breathing quietly for a while. Then she went home to George.

For more than a year, they waited for news about the case. Finally, one evening after dinner in January 2008, Darci was in the kitchen making sugar cookies with the kids, who were five and eighteen months. Someone knocked at the door. She stopped mixing the batter, opened the door, and found a skinny cop in his early twenties whom she'd seen around town. He was holding an arrest warrant. The paper was shaking in his hand. He said, "I really hate this."

He let Darci gather some clothes and kiss her kids before she walked out with him. George would have custody of the children. She was nervous and sobbing but trying to keep it together as much as she could. Again, part of her was relieved. She'd been waiting uncertainly, and now she no longer had to wait. The officer didn't even handcuff her—he gave her a cigarette on the way to the jail.

It turned out that in the few months she had been at Ferrellgas, she had stolen more than $13,000. It was an impossible sum. Court fees and fines would raise the total restitution she would be ordered to pay to more than $15,000. She was released on bond while her attorney—a local man fulfilling his public defender obligation—negotiated a plea agreement.

Darci spiraled downward fast. On the night before and morning of her court date, she took Xanax and downed most of a bottle of vodka. I found this hard to believe at first, but later I would see her drink two bottles of wine before noon and realize she had a high tolerance for alcohol. In court, she was supposed to be signing her plea agreement, when the bailiff charged over to her and said angrily, "What are you doing?"

She looked down and realized she had lit a cigarette in the middle of the courtroom. "What's the big deal? It's just a cigarette, it's not illegal," she said, barely slurring the words out.

The judge ordered her to serve ten days for contempt of court. After that, she pleaded guilty to felony theft of property and was sentenced to six years of probation, but the judge ordered her to go to a rehabilitation program for sixty days first. For the duration of her sentence, she couldn't move to a new house without checking in, she had to make regular appointments with her probation officer, she couldn't get into any more legal trouble, and she had to stay sober.

• • •

The stress of Darci's legal problems and probation only intensi-
fied the toxicity of her relationship with George. Every year she
spent with him, she told me, made it harder and harder to get
away. Other people told me that they'd seen her be abusive, both
verbally and physically, to George as well. This is something people commonly say about domestic abuse victims, a way to deflect
responsibility from the men, and it's hard to assess the truth of it.
It's possible that she was violent with George at times. Often
that's how women learn to defend themselves against long-term
abuse.

George had always managed to make her feel small, she told
me. "I don't know. I've been reading this book about insecurity,"
she said one day in the fall of 2015, after I picked her up from jail.
"I really think I was very insecure. . . . I turn to men to find my
own security."

I asked her if she loved George—if she ever had and still did. "I
don't know if I've even ever been in love," she said. "I don't know
if I was in love with him." Darci had been obsessed with dating
since high school, and I was amazed to hear this admission. I
thought of all my loves, the accidental ones, the destructive ones,
and finally the comfortable, affirming ones. I could not have done
without any of them—they'd all helped build a whole me.

But she'd built a long-term relationship on mutual destruction.
I found a temporary order of protection that Darci had applied
for against George in March 2012. The form asked what threats
George had made against her. She wrote that he had said, "I could
easily kill you and no one would ever find your body." The hand-
writing is hers, familiar to me from the notes we used to pass in
school, and at odds with the gravity of the words. "I swear to God
if you don't shut your fucking mouth," Darci's quote from him
continued, "I will kill you and it would be worth it to go to
prison." Some of George's cousins—also my cousins—served in

the local sheriff's office and with the city of Clinton police, all of which enhanced his threats. He told her his cousins would cover for him.

Under "Actual Physical Abuse or Harm," she listed what George had done to her: closed-fist punches in the forehead, even on the vagina, black eyes, bruises all over, knots. He'd talked about killing everyone, including himself. (The order of protection was ultimately dismissed without prejudice.)

She tried to leave George several times, she told me, but had nowhere to go. The county had a domestic violence shelter—its location secret—but she couldn't stay there indefinitely, and then where would she go? She had no money. Her mom was still working but earned only about $30,000 a year, and her stepdad was retired. The house on School Hill had sold for $67,000, and though that had supplemented their income for a time, Virginia, already raising Cody's son, had no money to spare.

Once when Maddie was little, Darci had struck out on her own, renting a little apartment on School Hill. But "keeping up with everything alone was just too much," she'd told me. "And George was always a good dad." He also helped her get drugs. Sometimes after he hit her, she told me, she would leave and walk down the side of the highway, furious, until she found a hotel room to stay in. Usually those rooms were occupied by men she knew. Sometimes they let her stay in exchange for sex or drugs. That's how she survived: she would leave one situation in which she was dependent on a man and get into another one.

Darci finally separated from George in 2012. She went into a rehab facility in Little Rock, the Dorcas House, and stayed for almost a year. George retained custody of Maddie and Kai until his meth use escalated, at which point Virginia and David stepped in again and obtained legal custody of them, when they were ten and six. Virginia, then in her late fifties, was raising all three of her grandchildren.

Darci's story was familiar to me from growing up, a story of women falling on bad times because men have control over them, spiritually and financially. Declining economic conditions are linked to increases in domestic abuse. That link is well known, but it's usually tied to male unemployment: unemployed men are simply at home more often to abuse their partners more. But in 2016, a team of sociologists from the Fragile Families and Child Wellbeing Study found that abuse and violence increased even when men weren't unemployed. All they needed was a fear of hard times, a feeling that they'd lost control over their finances and their place in the workforce. Men try to control their partners more when they feel they can't control anything else. In Darci and George's world, where people were losing jobs and the town was losing people, men felt there was little about their lives they could control, so they tried to control women. The isolation and stress from the Covid-19 lockdowns in 2020 made these trends even worse: surveys from the *American Journal of Emergency Medicine* and UN Women found an increase in domestic violence around the globe. In almost every metro area they studied, calls to hotlines and emergency room visits with wounds typical of domestic abuse happened more frequently.

George was in prison when I first returned to Arkansas. In 2015 he'd confessed to a handful of burglaries in Choctaw, a small community just south of Clinton where doctors, lawyers, and retirees live. He'd broken into the local Veterans of Foreign Wars office—VFWs had the only bars allowed in the county—and stolen about $300 in cash. Then he broke into a nearby home, found a safe, stole a necklace, gold coins, a set of collector spoons, and some tools, and took a bath in the upstairs bathroom.

After his prison term, he was in and out of jail for failing to pay his court fines. Then he entered a rehabilitation center in Bee Branch. It had been set up next to a new nondenominational church by a pastor who had himself suffered from addiction. The pastor thought drugs were Satan and had to be cast out. George got construction jobs through that program and earned enough that eventually he was out on his own.

I reached out to George in the winter of 2018. At first he said he didn't want to talk, knowing I wanted to ask him about his relationship with Darci. He said he'd left that part of his life behind him and didn't want to dredge it all up again. Then he asked me to call him. He wanted to assure me that he wasn't trying to ignore me or be mean to me. "I feel bad," he said, "like you're trying to reconnect with a long-lost cousin and I'm stopping you."

Though I was curious about his time with Darci, I was actually trying to reconnect with my dad's family. My mom had in a sense denied us a full understanding of our family and our history; she'd worn her snobbery against his family like a shield and thought she could protect us from whatever impulses or potential addictions we'd inherited from them. By the time I spoke to George, I'd heard from several cousins that my great-grandmother, my dad's father's mother, had tried to ensure, through her will, that her heirs would have access to the family land forever, that anyone who wanted to could make a home on the Mountain. It had meant as much to her as the Farm had meant to my mom's dad, but I'd never heard her story.

In the years after I reconnected with Darci, my partner, Samir, began to come home with me for visits, and we drove together in our old Subaru Forester down the roads leading to my dad's family's land. Like other roads that wind down the east side of the Mountain, this one was paved at first, but soon gives way to gravel, then dirt, dipping down into a valley and ending at the Archey

Fork, flowing toward town. Some of the shacks my dad's family had grown up in were still standing, barely, but others had been cleared out, and some of the more prosperous cousins had built big houses along the ridge, overlooking the mountains farther north. Next to the cemetery where most of my dad's extended family, the Pottses and Bigelows and Willoughbys, were buried, the Nature Conservancy had bought some abandoned land and turned it into a preserve. The river pooled there into a small swimming hole, remote and pristine, a milky-blue refuge surrounded by tree-lined ridges.

Samir is from Miami and lived in the D.C. area when I met him, but when he saw the Ozarks for the first time, he said the area reminded him of Colombia, where he spent five years of his childhood. I think we were both in awe of finding that untrammeled spot with its unexpected beauty, clean water, a bluff line of pancaked limestone. It turned out that I had no claim to any of my dad's family's land. In my dad's eagerness to flee his family, he'd signed quitclaim deeds to various cousins over the years, relinquishing what might have been his small portion. I wondered if he'd ever been sad that he'd let it go.

I told George that I wanted to get to know my family better, that my parents had kept me away from my dad's side, away from the Mountain.

"There's probably a good reason for that!" he said emphatically. "This town didn't suck you down the way it did some of us."

A few months later, in the summer, George called me back, ready to talk. I drove over to his house one afternoon and found him in a trailer in the middle of nowhere, off the highway and behind a cattle ranch. He came out to meet me on the front porch of his trailer. He was slim, wearing shorts, a T-shirt, and a baseball cap, and his face was covered in tattoos. One looked like a salamander draped over his eye, and I asked what it was. "Some things we don't need to talk about," he said. "It seemed important at the time. It's not important now."

The whole time we were talking, George sat on the edge of his loveseat, knee bouncing, hands clasped. He was anxious. "Satan's trying to get me back," he said. He'd called me because he thought talking to me might help him at that moment: he didn't want to get high, and speaking to me about his past could be a good distraction.

He was staying in the trailer alone because his last roommate had moved out. It was immaculately clean and bare except for a few pieces of furniture and looked almost unlived in. Above us, a ceiling fan whirred with a steady click behind George's graveled, mumbly, Southern voice.

George told me a little about his mountain family. "Dad would stay gone for days at a time, and that's all that she would worry about and think about," he said of his mom. "I think they were caught up in each other more than their kids." They lived in deep poverty. "Back then, you used to have food stamps, paper things," he said. "The mailman would pull up and honk the horn, and I knew we'd drink soda pop that day. Have flapjacks for breakfast."

On weekends when he was growing up, the adults would already be drinking before shooing the kids off to bed. Then he would smell what he later recognized as pot. When it was just pot, everything was okay. In fact, George still thought pot could be good for people, could open up one's mind spiritually. But when he got older, he started using crystal meth. At first, he just partied on weekends, but over time the drug changed. "Now, if you do it, you must have it to survive," he said. "I think the devil is so smart. It's chemically designed that if you don't have it, you don't function." Using meth made him calm at first, then paranoid, then dangerous, then emotional. I asked him what he meant by dangerous.

"No care for nobody," he said. "Paranoia just as bad, because you think all the crazy things, about people trying to get you. It just opens your mind up to where Satan just throws his handlebars on your brain."

When I asked him about Darci, he said he was upset that she told everyone in town he'd abused her, but also didn't deny it. He said he'd loved her, but she found ways to make him mad.

I told him I thought their relationship had been destructive, and he agreed. "Very destructive."

Soon after we spoke, George moved out of his trailer—which was easy, since he owned nothing—threw all his clothes into a backpack, and started hiking through the woods. He would post pictures of himself on Facebook, climbing through the mountains. The devil was trying to get him, he would say, but he was fighting. He apparently slept out there. In February 2019 one of his sisters, Crystal, filed a petition to have him involuntarily committed. "He was found outside my sister's house and he said he was tired of living and he had taken a bunch of pills," Crystal wrote. "He just travels around walking everywhere, from one spot to the next. He is homeless. He is always dirty." He was self-medicating with illegal drugs, and she had taken him to the emergency room, where they thought he might need dialysis. "I'm afraid someone will find him dead somewhere. He needs help." George would eventually be sent back to jail, back to rehab, then back to jail again, in an endless cycle.

14.

The Trouble

Drugs had been a steady part of Darci's life since she was a teenager. Among the people who partied with Darci when we were young, one young woman later went to law school and is now a successful attorney. Another young woman is a teacher who lives in a slightly bigger town with her healthy, happy family. Many of them left town eventually. Few were eager to talk to me on the record about the teenage partying. We tend to think of heavy drug use and alcoholism as progressive diseases that inevitably worsen over time unless there's a dramatic intervention, but that's not always true. The majority of people who have had a substance use disorder at some point in their lives recover from it, and just under half do so on their own, without outside treatment, according to the Recovery Research Institute at Massachusetts General Hospital. Many people who drink or use drugs heavily in their early adulthood, even those who party hard like Darci just stop doing it when they get older.

Darci's friends who'd lost touch with her assumed that she had left that life behind too. Our friend Erica Hurt had sneaked out with Darci as a teenager and partied as well. "I [was] following the same path and, you know, not making good choices," she told me. She dropped out of high school to become a manager at McDonald's and stayed in Clinton for a year, then decided she needed a change. Like Cassandra and unlike Darci, she decided to leave. When she was eighteen or nineteen, her parents moved to the tourist town of Branson, Missouri, farther north in the Ozarks. She followed, picking up jobs as a waitress and in retail. When that environment wasn't enough of a change, she moved to northern Georgia, near Augusta, where other relatives lived. In Georgia, she met and married a man, had a son, and divorced. Ultimately, she found work at the local sheriff's department, trained to become a police officer, and was promoted to head its white-collar crimes unit.

Erica disappeared from my life once she left town, but after I reconnected with Darci, I searched for a way to contact her too. When I finally found her cell number and called her, I was surprised to hear the adult voice on the other end. She sounded completely different from the goofy, funny friend who'd once played the group ditz. She sounded in charge of her life and her work and her future. She'd remarried, and she and her second husband had just built their own house with a pool. We spent about an hour talking and catching up.

When I told her I was writing a book about our hometown and Darci, Erica was surprised to learn about Darci's problems.

"Darci was always just a cool girl, I guess, she was always a popular, cool girl," she remembered. "I guess I kind of assume the same thing about everybody. People are married and have kids of their own and have maybe a boring job like I do." Erica thought the most important thing she had done early in her life was to get away from people and places who would have dragged her down.

People in Clinton who continue to use drugs do so in part because the people they rely on, their entire social network, are also users. Darci was isolated and alone, stuck in an abusive relationship, tenuously housed. It's impossible to separate her continued substance abuse from the place she lived.

• • •

The first time Darci felt addicted—that she couldn't live without drugs—was, she said, after she had Kai, around the time she took the job at Ferrellgas and started embezzling money. I might have placed the onset of her substance use disorder earlier, but she felt she'd been in control of her use until then. When Maddie was little, Darci still felt a certain freedom and held on to hope for a different future, but Kai's birth would make striking out on her own, with two children in tow, much harder. It meant she was in Clinton to stay. Only in retrospect did she realize that the mood that settled on her then was depression.

Soon after Kai was born, Darci had a minor car accident that injured her back and caused her back pain. She was referred to a pain clinic in Conway that prescribed methadone. They gave her a one-month supply that lasted only two weeks; she took too much and ran out too quickly. In that two-week lull between the last of the medicine and her prescription refill, she took every kind of drug to abate the pain, and soon she felt she was really in trouble. It was partly because she was buying these drugs between methadone prescriptions that she and George were always broke and she continued stealing from Ferrellgas.

Even as she found ways to stop taking methadone, though, her use of other substances escalated. When she couldn't get prescription painkillers, she turned to crystal meth, which was now always around Van Buren County. In the late 1990s and early 2000s, people began to manufacture it with the over-the-counter decongestant Sudafed, in mom-and-pop laboratories throughout the woods and valleys of the Ozarks. Suddenly it was everywhere.

At its peak, Arkansas had the second-highest rate of meth use in the country. Overall use dipped for a short time when laws on selling Sudafed changed in 2005. But in the years when Darci was searching for whatever drug she could find, the rates of use for Arkansas remained relatively high compared to the rest of the United States. People found ways around regulations, and new suppliers popped up. In the late 2000s and throughout the 2010s, use of meth continued to rise and set the stage for the opioid epidemic. During the same period, alcohol abuse increased as well. In 2019 a study in the journal *Alcoholism Clinical and Experimental Research* found that between 1999 and 2017, deaths attributable to alcohol increased by 50.9 percent and that the largest increases were in white women.[*]

In the 1980s, rapid disinvestment from America's cities, white flight into suburbs, rising crime, and punitive policing practices left primarily Black Americans living in urban centers and hence more vulnerable to drug epidemics, which sweep in after basic institutions abandon an area. Today vulnerable populations are spread beyond cities to rural parts of the country, as entire economies and societies collapse and people flee.

This is a particularly American disease. Rather than use our society's vast wealth and resources to lift all people up, we are letting more and more people fall down. It is in our country's DNA

[*] Addiction is now thought to be something like a learning disorder that hijacks the brain's reward circuitry. Dr. Nora Volkow at the National Institutes of Health writes that while addiction varies from individual to individual, widespread societal conditions can raise the chances of a whole population becoming addicted. "We will never be able to address addiction," she says, "without being able to talk about and address the myriad factors that contribute to it—biological, psychological, behavioral, societal, economic, etc." In 2019 the American Society of Addiction Medicine redefined addiction to reflect this new research, shifting some of the focus away from individual behavior. "By ignoring the underlying drivers of drug consumption, current interventions are aggravating its trajectory," a group of scholars wrote in a letter to the *American Journal of Public Health* in 2018. "'Suffering' may be a better focus for physicians than 'pain.' Others have argued for 'compassion.' Health care providers have a role in reducing suffering historically and ethically."

to blame societal failings on the individuals who suffer from them the most and to think of addiction as a personal moral failing and to ignore the societal conditions that drive it.

• • •

In the early days of our renewed friendship, Darci never said she had an addiction. She always referred to the drugs she took as medications, and they often were. She frequently received prescriptions for anti-anxiety medications from various doctors, including Xanax and drugs she had abused in the past. Even when she didn't have a prescription, she found ways to get those medicines. She always had access to painkillers.[*]

Darci's drug use was inseparable from her interactions with doctors. Our country's private, atomized healthcare system wasn't able to keep track of her or assess her growing problem. It made me wonder about the line between drugs and medicine, and between need and addiction. I wanted to see her medical records, so on one of my visits, we went to two different doctors' offices and the local hospital, where Darci signed forms giving them permission to provide me with copies of her records going back to when she was eighteen. When the medical records arrived a few days later, there were so many pages they filled a moving box. I gave copies to Darci and frequently combed through them, slowly absorbing their account of Darci's life.

They were often emotionally hard to read. At times, they are a history of her most desperate moments. She took a lot of medications even when she was young, from antidepressants to anti-seizure medications, almost all of which were, at some point or

---

[*] In Arkansas, doctors wrote 93.5 prescriptions for opioid painkillers for every one hundred people.

another, popular for getting high. Many of them were market-able, and she had resold them. Darci also went to doctors fre-quently, with even minor complaints: she fell when she put on her jeans and hurt her foot; her daughter poked her in the eye; she had a cold and a sore throat. She once went to a doctor because she'd had too much coffee and felt "jacked up" after drinking it. She said she had a lot of car accidents after swerving to miss dogs or road debris. She said she fell a lot. She went once with two black eyes. After she had a physical altercation with a person she wouldn't name, she called an ambulance, and the paramedics found her sitting in the middle of a road.

What struck me most was that she was frequently seeing doc-tors and nurses because of emotional pain. Many of the records recorded Darci's accounts of things that had happened to her, along with plainspoken assessments from the healthcare profes-sional she was speaking to. Some of them sound like they come from a concerned observer who knew Darci well. In such a small town, it's possible they did. I found these observers' matter-of-fact records of her distress unsettling. "Honestly she looks better than other times I've seen her in the past," a nurse wrote when Darci was twenty-six, indicating a lightly rendered judgment. When she came into the office sobbing with baby Kai on her hip, "she was crying most of visit stating 'I just don't know what to do' . . . 'I have 2 kids at home and I have to take care of them' . . . later asking for a shot for pain 'for ride home.'"

The records also showed her history of depression. When she was twenty-four, her mom and stepdad brought her to the emer-gency room. "Has some scratches on L wrist in a simulated (not serious) attempt," the nurse wrote. I asked Darci about it, and she told me she had been trying to kill herself. It was devastating to see her pain confirmed in such bureaucratic language. "Denies suicidal ideation," several other records noted. Darci didn't seek psychotherapy. There weren't many therapists in town anyway. Many people in Clinton still associated therapy with serious mental disorders—Darci did—and their knowledge of mental health treatment came from knowing people who in extreme distress had been sent unwillingly to state hospitals. In those years, Darci wouldn't have known where to go for help except to medical doctors, who could really only ask her if she was suicidal, to which she would say no.

Her doctors' visits and drug use escalated dramatically after Kai was born. Something seemed to change for her, just as she'd remembered, a shift in her use and addiction.

The records were given to me in chronological order, with the most recent on top and the oldest at the bottom. The older records, from when she was nineteen and twenty, were handwritten or typed, faint and harder to read. I skimmed through them at first. It felt like an accident when I paused to read one from 2000 with the following note: "Darci is here stating that she is having trouble with anxiety." I noted the strange, familiar use of the first name. "She describes a virtual cascade of family tragedies stating that her grandmother recently died, her grandfather's health has deteriorated. She is also stating a past history of her best friend dying in a car wreck in 1998."

It stopped me cold, because I knew she meant Ashley.

Ashley hadn't been Darci's best friend. I had been her best friend. Ashley was my sister. I felt an angry flash: Darci had used Ashley's tragedy to get drugs by making the nurse feel sorry for her. I tried to envision Darci's life back in Clinton then and fit that in: *She used the death of my sister to feed her drug habit.* I was furious. I read the passage again and again.

The day Ashley died, she had three friends with her, and I had avoided them as assiduously as I'd avoided anyone else in the years since I left Clinton. One of them developed a serious drug problem in high school and was later diagnosed with bipolar disorder. When I ran into this girl in town, she scolded me because she'd found Ashley's grave uncleaned, unweeded, uncared for. "She deserves better than that, she was really special," her friend would tell me in a semicoherent ramble. Neither my mom nor I had the heart to go out there, but I did visit Ashley's grave once and found a shiny toy windmill sticking out of the ground, the kind we used to get from dollar stores. I knew from the look of it that this friend must have left it. People told me the town went easier on her because of Ashley's death. "Oh, they'd say, you know her death was really hard on her," another of Ashley's friends told me. "But you know, at some point, you have to stop that." When the friend ended up in jail for drug use, Momma went down to see her and told her to stop blaming Ashley's death for her problems. It didn't work.

What would it have been like if I'd stayed in town and been confronted, every day after Ashley's death, with the memories of her, the places she'd been, and the people she'd known? The high school she would never graduate from? Clinton would have required me to mourn her in the short-circuited way, missing her no longer than it took me to remember that she was in heaven and that I'd see her again someday. I did not share that belief. "It was just God's plan," people would say. But Darci and some of Ashley's other friends had gotten mired in it. I'd dealt with the trauma by moving, which didn't make my mourning process any less legitimate. After I left, other young people had died: another girl from our class, in a drunken driving incident; a classmate who'd had a heart attack at the age of thirty-four, from drug use; a suicide; another heart problem from drug use. Some of them I didn't know. Darci knew all of them. Doctors call what Darci was doing—hopping from one office to another looking for prescriptions—drug-seeking behavior. But that doesn't mean that Darci wasn't trying to treat real pain.

• • •

In March 2008, when Darci was put on probation for stealing the money from Ferrellgas, she was supposed to stop using any drug she didn't have a prescription for, and she was subjected to regular drug tests. Her original probation term ought to have ended after six years, in 2014, about a year before we reconnected. But it didn't, because she had continued violating her probation, especially by testing positive for drug use throughout. At various times, her probation officer would recommend that she enter a treatment facility. There were a few rehabilitation centers around the state then; most were only for thirty days of treatment. Darci went through drug treatment programs three times before I met up with her again and almost always left them and immediately began using again.

She stayed longest in Dorcas House, in Little Rock. It's a Christian-based recovery center that also works with victims of domestic violence. (The director of the program, Dorcas Vanglist, told me that almost all the women there had a history of sexual trauma or domestic abuse in addition to substance use disorders: the two often go hand in hand.) Darci entered in 2012, and she was there for seven months. She did well for a while, earning privileges and gaining trust, but then she started taking a prescription cold medicine containing a substance called dextromethorphan to get high. She had seen a parental warning label on a box of DayQuil, she told me, which had sparked her curiosity and led her to experiment. She knew it wouldn't pop up on tests, but it was obvious to everyone she was taking something. ("Darci is not a nice person when she uses, as you may have noticed," Vanglist told me. I knew some of what she was talking about, but I hadn't seen the worst of it: yelling, screaming, crying, and cruelty to whoever was closest to her.) After she started to get high there, she lost privileges and got in ever more trouble.

Darci became frustrated, and early in the summer, she walked out of Dorcas House and called a friend for a ride to Clinton. She stayed with different people around town. While the weather was warm, she lived in a tent at a Greers Ferry Lake campground. It was at this time that Virginia and David went to court for official legal guardianship of Maddie and Kai, of whom George still had legal custody. Darci told me she'd left Dorcas House so she could help with their guardianship case. "Maybe Darci thought that was true in her mind," Virginia told me, but it wasn't so.

She stopped reporting to her probation officer and was marked as absconded from her program. By that fall, when the police caught up with her, she'd violated her probation so many times that the court finally canceled it altogether and charged her with the new crime of violating it. She was found guilty in early 2014 and sentenced to three years in prison.*

Darci served less than a year of her sentence, with credit for time served, split between the county jail and a prison in the southern part of the state. She was released in April 2014 to live at her mom's place. A year later she reached out to me on Facebook, and she was still living there, and still on parole, when I first met up with her again.

When Darci absconded from her drug treatment program,

---

* Incarcerated women are likely to have been living in poverty and to have compounding problems, like a history of domestic abuse and substance use disorders. Sixty percent of incarcerated women have minor children. When they're released, they face barriers to finding employment and housing, and separation from their children.

she'd been on the county's "most wanted" list. Her mug shot had run in the county paper, and in 2013 a friend sent it to me via Facebook Messenger. The friend said she had taught Maddie in school. Darci's "life from what I could tell was one big mess when we had the little girl in pre-K," the friend said. "Don't know if she will ever get on the right path—let's hope so for those kids' sake!" Other people had expressed similar sentiments: that it was hard to see Darci around town with her kids in tow, her life a mess. They felt sorry for her children for having to deal with that. No one ever seemed to regret Darci's troubles for her own sake. It had already occurred to me that people like those I had grown up with were dying because the world around them was falling apart. But only then did I realize why it had all fallen so hard on women: they were still expected to be the nurturers in spite of everything. They were supposed to keep the community going, through their thankless service to the next generation, the children to whom everyone turned for hope for a better future, no matter the status of their own lives. Women were held morally responsible for everything that happened in their families and communities. They were supposed to sacrifice everything for their children, even their own happiness and mental health.

15.

The Trailer

When Darci spoke to me about her life, she spoke as though the worst was over, especially after she left George. She identified as a survivor of domestic abuse, and she told her story often. I knew that wasn't the entire truth. She also had a substance use disorder, and two pre-teen children who were in the custody of her aging mother, who was also taking care of Darci's nephew. Virginia ought to have been thinking about retiring, but instead she was still working, picking up the pieces her grown children had left behind. It would lead to problems of her own.

My cousin Wesley Potts was an investigator at the sheriff's department. When I visited him, he remembered Darci—he'd often been called out to break up fights between her and George. One thing he said stayed with me: being sober must be devastating to someone like Darci. "Can you imagine waking up in your life, at thirty-five, and realizing you have nothing?" he asked me. In his experience, people with addictions crash hardest after they've seen their lives during a period of clarity. So I should have been prepared for what happened to Darci.

On Darci's thirty-fifth birthday, I flew back home to northern Virginia. On my way to the airport in Little Rock, I went to say goodbye to her, and we chatted in the driveway of her mom's house. We hugged and promised to keep in touch, and this time we meant it. A few days later, settled back in my Washington, D.C., suburb, I got a call from Darci's mom. Virginia told me that after I left for the airport, Darci had taken Xanax, the anti-anxiety drug, which always made her combative and angry. She'd gone downtown and met up with someone she was prohibited from seeing because they were both on parole. The two got into a fight in the middle of the courthouse square. Someone in town called the police, and Darci was arrested. In her mugshot, she's wearing the headband I'd last seen her in, but her face looks old. It's set in a disgruntled frown, and her eyes look mean. Later, she'd call that the "Darci face," as a joke; it was the face she made when she was angry, upset, and usually high.

I was heartbroken that I hadn't been there and wouldn't be anytime soon. She'd picked such a public place to get into trouble—the courthouse square, where we'd walked when we were catching up. It's not far from the police station, so in fighting there, she'd almost guaranteed that she'd be arrested. Virginia said Darci was in the county jail and would stay there until she was transported to a program for parole violators in Pine Bluff. She was held in Pine Bluff throughout the summer of 2015.

I didn't visit Darci in jail that spring or summer. I had to apply to visit, and then she had to initiate a long process for the application on her end, and by the time it was approved, in mid-August, her release date was near. So I arranged to go with Virginia to pick her up on September 1, 2015. Pine Bluff is about two hours from Clinton, on the other side of Little Rock. Virginia didn't like to drive on the interstate, so she was happy when I offered to drive.

Virginia and I talked a lot about Darci during the drive. I asked if she and the kids were ready for Darci's return. "Kai is happy, because he loves his momma," she told me. He had just turned nine that summer. "Maddie's not really excited about her mom coming back home. It's because of what she's seen as long as she can remember, especially in the last year." This surprised me because I thought Darci had had a good year. Maddie "doesn't have any respect for her mother, is what it is. I don't know how we're going to deal with that." Maddie, at almost thirteen, was getting more aware of family problems. "I'm hoping it will be better this time."

I asked Virginia if she was ready for Darci to come home. "Not really," she said. "We've been praying." Though she would have liked to hear Darci's voice over the phone, she had never set up the system to do so because it cost too much money.* In her letters, Darci had said she was doing better, that she understood she had problems and was trying to solve them. Virginia was hopeful but not naïve.

When we arrived at Pine Bluff, we started to get out of the car, but a guard yelled, "Stay in your vehicle!" We jumped back inside and laughed nervously, unsure exactly what to do. Had we gotten into trouble for doing something wrong? The directions for picking up Darci had been vague and confusing, so we sat in the car, waiting anxiously, for nearly an hour.

Darci appeared at the big metal gate at last. We had to stay in the car and drive closer before the guard would let her out. She looked happy, waving and smiling, wearing the same loose floral clothing she'd worn on her birthday, when I'd last seen her.

---

* Telephone rates from prisons and jails are notoriously high, an issue that has long been a focus of advocates. Nationwide the average cost of a fifteen-minute call from a jail is $5.74, but in some states it's almost five times that with setup fees and other charges, according to the Prison Policy Initiative. The Federal Communications Commission capped some rates in some facilities in May 2021.

When she made it out to us, she practically bounded into the car. She seemed relieved and incredibly normal. In the past, she typically spoke in a half-formed way, as if she couldn't quite hold on to words before they slipped out. Maybe it was from drug use. But right out of jail, her voice was clear, if a bit raspy—she was still a smoker—and her sentences were crisp. *Sober,* I thought in a flash.

On the drive back, Virginia told Darci, "Kai has been counting the days." Was he still taking martial arts lessons downtown? Darci asked eagerly. Yes, he was still doing karate. "Good," Darci said. "I like that for him. It gives him confidence." Kai also liked his teacher and the new principal.

What was Maddie doing in school? Darci asked. Virginia said she was doing pep squad and was a bit of a mean girl. Also, Darci's nephew had broken up with his girlfriend, but they got back together.

Darci moved back into Virginia and David's house, to her couch in the living room. I stayed in Clinton for another week and visited her often. I went with her once to Kai's practice. He hurt his thumb and came over to her, holding his hand up, wounded and upset. Darci said, "Ooohhhh, it's okay, bud," sympathetically, kissed his thumb, ruffled his hair, and let him sit with us for the rest of the practice. I often saw her like this with Kai: playful and nurturing. She took him to the playground and pushed the merry-go-round with him, her floral skirts billowing in the air, her face up to the sun. Wherever we were, he stayed near her, eager, affectionate, always happy to have her around. Maddie was more withdrawn and suspicious.

Virginia and David still had custody of Maddie and Kai, and Virginia had done the day-to-day mothering of them for most of their lives. Darci had told me her goal was to live with her kids again and become their legal guardian, but she was running out of time to make that a reality.

Darci had hated her time in the parole violators program. "It's like a mental boot camp," she told me. It had been grueling and dehumanizing. That was when she showed me the mug shot taken at the time of her arrest on the courthouse square. "I look so crazy," she said. "I keep it to remind myself not to be that person again." She sounded sincere, and I believed her. But then, I had never heard that speech before.

. . .

Despite Darci's resolve, her life spiraled out of control soon after she returned home. One afternoon in November, Virginia, David, and the kids all left for Texas, to visit David's family. While they were gone, Darci would stay in town with a friend. But after they'd gone, Darci realized she'd left her phone in their house. She went to retrieve it and found all the doors locked. She didn't have a key, so she broke a window to get into the house. She told me later she'd been high. A few days later David and Virginia returned to find the window smashed and the house broken into, and they realized Darci had done it. They kicked her out of their home and told her she wouldn't be welcome there again.

I'd returned to northern Virginia by then and found Darci difficult to reach by phone or message. She rarely had a phone or prepaid minutes available. She would disappear for long stretches and change her number often. I didn't know she was no longer in Virginia's house.

When I did find her again, it was on that Christmas Eve at James's house, on Bee Branch Mountain, and she was drunk at ten in the morning.

After we drove away from James's trailer, the dogs milling about in the driveway behind us, I asked Darci what had happened, but she wouldn't quite finish the story, and I had to figure it out later. She was angry at her mom and her stepdad for kicking her out of the house and upset to be apart from her kids, but also didn't think she would go back to live there. She worked through her conflicting emotions out loud.

Darci was thinking about how quickly Virginia had gotten together with David after her first stepdad's death. "She was so vulnerable," Darci told me. "It goes back a generation because her mom was kind of the same way. . . . If she has a man there taking care of her, her children are kind of the second priority. I don't mean that against my mom. . . . It's like a yucky understanding, and it's just her lot." She thought Virginia had never had the opportunity to discover who she really was and what she really wanted. I thought this applied to Darci as well.

When Darci had first asked me to drive her to Little Rock that Christmas Eve, she'd been vague about the errand she needed to run, but I'd agreed anyway. Once we were on our way, she told me she needed to go to the Dorcas House, in Little Rock. After her parents kicked her out of their house, she had begged the Dorcas House director to take her back. But she'd lasted only two weeks there, and now they had bags of her clothes and belongings that she needed to pick up.

I asked why she'd left Dorcas House. She tried to tell me she'd left of her own accord: "The final straw was when my roommates were continuing to sneak heroin in, and I didn't do it and had no desire to." But when we arrived at Dorcas House—a big two-story brick house—it was clear to me she'd gotten into trouble there. Staff and volunteers, who gathered in the front hallway to see her, told her the administration might give her another chance and advised her to "just let this blow over." When I asked her what they'd meant, she looked chagrined, laughed, and didn't give me a straight answer.

In the meantime, people working in the office, who were mostly Dorcas House clients fulfilling a work duty for their treatment program, brought out half a dozen trash bags filled with Darci's clothes. Darci ignored them, just kept chatting and visiting, and I realized I was the one who was going to carry the bags to the car. They weren't heavy, but there were a lot of them. I piled them onto a dolly and rolled them outside. Eventually, Darci joined me, and we drove back to Bee Branch Mountain.

At James's, the men and I took the bags out of the car, still without her help. I couldn't get back into the car fast enough. It was already four-thirty, well past the time I'd planned to be home, and my family was waiting for me for Christmas Eve dinner. I was frustrated and a little angry: I'd done her the favor of driving her, but she'd completely ignored my request for us to get home in time for my mom to run Christmas Eve errands. But then she stopped me in the muddy yard and took a deep breath in, her eyes reddening, suddenly emotional that we were saying goodbye. She hugged me, and when I pulled back, I was surprised to see her crying. I told her I'd see her soon.

Only after I left did it sink in that while I was going to spend Christmas with family, she was stuck with random men she didn't really know, estranged from her parents and children, drunk on a mountain, with all her belongings stuffed into trash bags. I knew she missed her family, but she'd been at home and safe with her kids before she'd messed it up, so I blamed her a bit. Was James using her? Or was she using James? Had she been using me? I didn't know the answers, and my heart hurt for her, but I wanted to return to my family, waiting for me in my mom's house.

Darci had not been completely honest with me about where she

was in her life when we'd first met up. She'd said she was past relying on men who mistreated her, and was done using, and was
looking forward to a return to a more stable life, one that involved
getting her own place and having her kids return to live with her
so that she could be a mom to them again. In our earlier meetings,
she had told me she planned to return to school so she could become a social worker.

It would take some time for me to reckon with the panic I'd
felt from the moment I'd first set foot in James's trailer. I didn't
want to judge her for being at James's, but I had to recalibrate
my expectations for her and for us as friends. Something about
the trailer was hard to handle. Here was my childhood best
friend living in my own worst nightmare, stuck in a trailer in
rural Arkansas, fifteen minutes from the hometown we'd both
hated so much growing up. Much later, I would regret leaving
her there.

I'd recorded our conversation on the way home from Little
Rock, with her permission, and when I listened to it again, I was
surprised at how much of it I'd missed. I discovered, amid the
rambling, that Darci had tried to talk about Ashley. She'd given
Maddie "Ashley" as a middle name. "I try to show her and tell her
stories about our childhoods," she said, "about Ashley, because, I
tell her, her middle name has a meaning. That's why she has that
name."

After a silence, she'd asked, "Are you ever going to have kids,
Monica?" I told her I didn't know, and it might be too late.
"If you don't, will you, will you become Maddie's godmother?
Maybe?"

When I heard that again, I started to sob, both because she'd
asked and because I'd been too wrapped up in my frustrations
to hear her. She wasn't as aware as I was about the research on

deaths of despair and about women like her who were dying younger and younger. She didn't seem aware of how precarious her life was. But she must have had some sense of what was happening, because, at thirty-five, she was finding her own way to prepare to die.

• • •

When I went back home to Virginia after that brief trip, Darci became hard to find again. In January 2016, I started to receive strange, nonsequitur notes from her on Facebook Messenger. "My heart [is] absolutely aching not from the breaking and bending though. It is an honest, healthy ache that is a healing pain," she texted me, completely out of the blue. "I know because it has happened, when I've allowed it several times over the past 3yrs since I left George after 11 yrs. Here's"—the message ended there, abruptly. Later she checked in to see if I'd understood her message, which I hadn't: "Its just a bit of me telling about when I finally left George Did u get it?"

I sent a bunch of frantic responses, asking what had happened. I told her I was worried she seemed down. "Down is one way to put it," she responded. "James turned out to be a nightmare in redneck hell I made out alive but it got really bad. And so goes the journey of my life. We will talk soon and I will fill u in."

I didn't hear from her again for weeks. Only later did I learn what happened to her next from our childhood friend Vanessa. Vanessa had returned to Arkansas from Colorado six years earlier when her marriage ended, and she'd lost her young son in a car accident. She'd suffered years of abuse and her husband had struggled with drugs.

After this tragedy, Vanessa had moved into a cabin behind the new house her parents had built in Choctaw. She'd enrolled her daughter in Clinton High School and had another son, with another friend of ours from high school. They still lived separately then, and Vanessa stayed alone in her quiet cabin with her daughter and infant son, mourning her loss and finding a new peace.

That January Vanessa was in a gas station in Choctaw when she ran into Darci, beaten and bloody and carrying a trash bag full of clothes. She had left the trailer on Bee Branch Mountain but had nowhere to go, so Vanessa invited her to her cabin to sleep on the couch.

That night Vanessa awoke to the sounds of slamming cabinet doors. She found Darci in the kitchen rummaging through her cabinets. "I'm hungry," Darci said.

Vanessa told her she could help herself to anything she needed, then tried to go back to sleep. But for the rest of the night, Darci's noises kept her awake. Darci had whispery phone calls with someone, perhaps a lot of people, from the couch, and didn't sleep at all.

Vanessa was sure she was high, the jittery, tweaking high people get from meth. The next day she told her she wasn't welcome in her cabin and asked her to leave. Vanessa told me she loved Darci and wished her the best, but she didn't feel comfortable having her around her kids.

Darci had nowhere to go. She couldn't go back to James's trailer. She still had nearly two years left on her parole, which meant she was still supposed to comply with its terms—no breaking laws, no using illegal drugs, no being with fellow ex-offenders—and consistently attend appointments with her supervising officer. She wasn't doing any of those things.

Darci stayed with various friends. Then in February, she went back to the gas station in Choctaw where Vanessa had found her a few weeks before. She went into the bathroom and didn't come out, so the clerk called the police. Paramedics responded, too, and took her to the hospital.

At some point, Darci told them she was tired from being homeless. "Patient denies suicidal/homicidal ideation," the doctor wrote. "States she is homeless and was in the bathroom at Choctaw station because she was nauseated. Report from EMS stated patient had been in bathroom two hours, spoon with residue found in bathroom. Patient denies using or shooting up drugs. Patient denies suicidal/homicidal numerous times. Parole officer has informed sheriff's office." Virginia told me that when the officers showed up to take her to jail for violating her parole, Darci told them she was ready to go.

Darci was sent to another program for parolees who violated the terms of their release, this time in Fayetteville, the booming college town in the northwestern corner of the state. It was her second trip to such a facility in six months and my first glimpse of the cyclical nature of Darci's life. Over the following years, this would be her rhythm: release, decline, imprisonment, release. How Darci was doing depended on where she was in that cycle. The first time I went through one with her, I was hopeful we would break her out of it. But it wasn't long before I wondered if anyone ever escaped cycles like these.

Darci and I wrote letters to each other while she was in the Fayetteville prison. Whenever she was in a facility, she was in a hopeful phase, swearing next time would be different, swearing her life was changed. "There's so much to tell you that's happened since we last spoke," she wrote. "But, it'll be so much easier to tell you most of it when we speak again. Basically, I ended up getting caught up with a bunch of people doing some bad things—namely, meth—and here I am. I can honestly say, though, I'm glad I got arrested when I did because I went from bad to the worst I'd ever been, so fast that there's no telling where I would have ended up."

16.

Moving

George's sister Crystal had also had a substance use disorder and a long history of legal problems. In 2013 she kidnapped her ex-boyfriend and held him at gunpoint. This resulted in several charges that sent her to prison. When she was released, she entered a faith-based recovery program. It worked for her, and she became very religious, keeping her hair long and wearing skirts. She started to attend an apostolic church in town, inside an old mechanic's garage on the highway. She was a Holy Roller, Darci's kids said.* Part of the problem with Clinton and rural Arkansas in general was that, since almost all the programs available to people with substance use disorders were faith based, the only tales of success that people had were through religion. It reaffirmed what they were already inclined to believe, that the only way to seek help was through God.

That was what people wanted from Darci. They wanted her to get clean with religious help. They wanted her to be a mother again. Mutual friends asked me how she was doing, but they didn't want her back in their lives. "I like her, I always have," people would tell me. "It's a shame she's not doing better."

Darci's parole ended and she was released in September 2016.

---

* I requested interviews with Crystal, but she declined.

She enrolled in a small, faith-based rehabilitation program in Green Forest, in northwestern Arkansas, near the tourist town of Eureka Springs. Green Forest is about the same size as Clinton, but its proximity to larger towns gives it a different feel: busier, with more of a future.

The rehab center, Jeremiah House, accommodated a half-dozen women at a time. It had been opened a few years before by Vickie Poulson, a woman whose personal experience with meth went deep. Both her husband and her daughter had recovered from addictions. After her mother died, Vickie inherited her house and decided to turn it into a home for women who were in recovery situations. She wanted it to be a place for those who were already well on the road to recovery, a safe place to launch the next period of their lives. She didn't expect them to work for their first three months there, and they could stay for up to two years: it was a wealth of time in the recovery world, and Vickie knew they needed it.

Vickie enrolled in several state certification programs to study addiction recovery. She believed in medicine-based recovery and had seen good results with the drug Suboxone for people with addictions to opioids. This was rare in Arkansas: most people were suspicious of using medicine, believing that it traded one addiction for another. Most programs were solely faith based. Jeremiah House was also faith based, and Vickie's husband, J.R., was a pastor in a nondenominational church next door called Soul Purpose, but she knew recovery was hard work and required a multipronged approach.

I went to see Darci there in April 2017, on Easter weekend, soon after she was allowed nonfamily visitors. I found her in the yard of Jeremiah House, sitting on a purple bench. Several benches encircled the yard, emblazoned with the Christian Twelve Steps.

"This program is just different," she told me hopefully. "I feel different. It feels right to be out of Clinton, and I feel better." She missed her kids—Maddie was fourteen and Kai was eleven—who were both still living with Virginia and David, but she thought it was good to have some space to get herself well. She had a job at a deli counter at a grocery store nearby and had enrolled in classes at a community college in Harrison, about thirty minutes away.

For Easter weekend, Vickie and J.R. had planned an around-the-clock song and prayer program, beginning on Good Friday and ending at sunrise on Easter Sunday. Vickie called the event "The Soaking," a full saturation of worship. That weekend Soul Purpose was full of worshippers coming in and out, including women from Jeremiah House and a handful of women who had already graduated from the program or knew Vickie from her work at other centers.

The church was an old single-room chapel, with a few offices in the back. We entered through the back door and passed J.R.'s office. Signs on the walls said things like DON'T LOOK DOWN ON ANYONE, UNLESS YOU'RE STOPPING TO HELP THEM UP. J.R. had long hair and a beard and wore khakis and T-shirts. One of Darci's fellow parishioners told me that once while she was working her shift at Walmart, he'd come in, and she'd pointed him out to a co-worker. Her co-worker commented that he didn't look like a preacher. "That's why I like him!" the parishioner said. He wasn't too buttoned up, and he didn't judge.

About half a dozen people flowed in and out of the small chapel—women with tattoos and sunbaked skin, women who looked older than they were because of years of smoking and drugs. Many were sprawled on the floor, making art with crayons and colored pencils on paper strewn about on the tattered red carpet. People closed their eyes and raised their hands to the exposed wooden beams of the ceiling and sang along to the steady lineup of Christian music that the bands were playing.

Darci and I sat in the front pew to watch one of the bands, a group of three women. One played a keyboard while the other two sang the same chorus over and over. The songs were simple and repetitive, easy to memorize quickly and repeat, and most of the crowd sang along. It felt like we were in a sort of collective meditation.

I looked over at Darci. Her eyes were closed, and she was swaying back and forth, a half smile on her face. Her hands were clasped in front of her T-shirt. She hummed a little. Vickie came over, hugged her, and said, "This is the song I want you to learn! I can't wait to hear you sing it." Darci's singing voice is clear and sweet, but it also has a subdued quality. She is less confident as a singer than as a person, as if singing means too much to her, because it bridges her real life to the dream life, the music career that might have been. Her timid voice rose up singing in the church beside me. I tried to swallow and, staring at the wooden rafters, started crying instead, from the beauty of the music, the moment, the good feelings about Darci for that brief spell.

Darci noticed I was crying. She smiled, and I put my hand on my chest. "I don't know why I'm so emotional," I said, and laughed.

"It happens." She patted my leg, then pointed beside me. "There's tissues right there."

Darci's plan was to stay at Jeremiah House, earn a degree, and get an apartment so that her children could come visit. It seemed like too much to take on so quickly. That afternoon, though, she seemed like her old self. We laughed and talked for hours.

Afterward Vickie sounded a note of caution. "Darci likes to talk the talk," she said. "But I haven't seen her demonstrate that she's able to do all the things she wants to do yet."

When I got home, I worried about her. What would derail her this time? I wondered. Would it be pills, or men?

It was pills.

Darci stayed in Jeremiah House through the spring of 2017. I visited her there several times. On one visit, in June, as we chatted, Vickie came in, furious. Darci's room was a mess. Funders were coming to tour the house in a few minutes, and all the residents were supposed to keep their areas tidy. I left then, and Darci went to her job at the grocery store.

Later that evening, after work, Darci returned to the group home, where Vickie confronted her at an impromptu meeting with the other residents. Vickie asked her to empty out her purse. Darci refused at first, but eventually opened it up. Inside were two empty cold medicine packets. This was a transgression Vickie couldn't overlook—women who stayed at Jeremiah House were supposed to be sober. Darci had already broken many other house rules.

Vickie made Darci a generous offer: she could have a bed at another rehabilitation facility for thirty days to get sober again. In the meantime, Vickie would hold her bed at Jeremiah House and let her come back when she was ready.

Darci refused. She told Vickie that she had made so much progress at school and at her job that she didn't want to take a step back.

"We love her and will continue to pray for her daily," Vickie wrote to me later. "I'm sure she could use a friend right now."

That night Darci went to a small motel down the road from Jeremiah House, where people lived for a weekly fee of about $140. It had a full-size bed, a bathroom, a tiny kitchenette with a refrigerator and a microwave, and not much else.

I found her there a few days later, surrounded by cheap wood paneling, sitting on an uncomfortable, scratchy bedspread. Vickie had moved most of her belongings out of her room at Jeremiah House and into a storage unit a few blocks away. A friend from

Soul Purpose was on his way that afternoon with his truck to help her get her things.

Sitting on the edge of the bed, Darci told me about being kicked out. She remained hopeful and positive about her future. She was enrolled in college for the coming fall semester, which would begin in mid-August, and planned to get a ride to class from some of her friends who were still at Jeremiah House. "I've been in bad places before, and this is not it," she reassured me. "I can do this and I feel really good about it." She kept saying this, over and over. I believed that she believed it.

I asked her about the cold medicine. "I've always been good at chemistry," she told me offhandedly, and explained how she'd learned how to combine over-the-counter medicines to achieve what she was looking for.

"Are you using them to get high?" I asked, confused.

"I haven't taken anything to get high for a long time," she said. She paused then and clasped her hands. She pursed her lips to keep from crying. She looked out the window and made a few false starts. "I—" she would start, then look off into the distance, trying to decide what to say and how to say it.

But whatever revelation or admission was about to follow, it was interrupted. The friend who had offered to help haul her things from storage knocked on the door. She introduced us, and we all drove together to the storage unit and started throwing her plastic bags into the back of his red pickup. Plastic bags, again.

17.

The Downward Spiral

My partner, Samir, and I moved from the D.C. suburbs to Clinton late in 2017. We moved for several reasons, not least of which was that I'd started to feel at home in Clinton again. I thought it would be easier to keep in touch with Darci if I were nearby. But by the time we moved back, she was slowly disappearing from my life again.

Even after she was kicked out of Jeremiah House, Darci kept her job at the grocery store deli counter for a couple of months, walking to work or getting rides for her shift. (Her ride to the community college had fallen through, and she had withdrawn for the fall semester.) In August, she qualified for an apartment in Green Forest for low-income residents so that her rent would only be sixty dollars. She moved in and found free furniture and other assistance, mostly through charities.

Once she was in the apartment, she fell into a deep depression and took to sleeping all the time. After several no-calls and no-shows at her job, her supervisors called the police to make sure she was still alive. The officers found her in her bedroom. She already had a history of being late to work and struggling to finish tasks during her shifts. Her bosses reviewed her case and fired her about a week after the wellness check.

I visited her often in the fall of 2017 and early winter of 2018. I stayed over one night, and we watched movies and had a little picnic of cheese, sausages, fruit, and wine. Her kids came to visit her occasionally, and she told me that they'd have slumber parties, making blanket pallets on the floor and watching movies until late.

I worried about Darci. She was incredibly lonely. She'd applied for unemployment but was rejected because she'd been fired. She couldn't find another job and borrowed money from Virginia that her mother couldn't spare. In the spring semester, Darci re-enrolled in online courses at her community college. Her scholarships and grants and loans added up to $2,000 more than tuition, an amount that she received as a stipend check. She used half of it to buy a 1998 Honda Accord. She never attended any of the online classes.

In early 2018, she'd promise to drive down to Clinton to visit us, but she rarely showed up. If she did, she'd arrive several hours later than planned. Her scholarship money quickly ran out, and she asked Virginia for gas and grocery money. The minute Virginia sent it through cash apps on her phone—twenty dollars, sixty dollars, whatever she could—Darci would claim it had already been spent and that she needed more. Then she missed Kai's twelfth birthday party. It was held at a pool in Fairfield Bay, the retirement resort town near us, and that morning Darci promised that she was already on the road and would arrive in time. Toward the end of the party, Kai swam over to Virginia and asked where his mom was. When Virginia said she didn't know, she told me, he shrugged and said, "She probably didn't have any money."

Sometimes I found her high—later she told me she was taking meth—in her bed in the middle of the day. She would talk in an endless stream of consciousness that made only occasional sense. I would ask if she wanted to come outside with me, and she'd say no. She stopped initiating contact. She tended to drift away from me when her life became complicated. Maybe it was because she didn't entirely trust me. Maybe she thought I would judge her. Thinking she needed space or privacy, I decided to give it to her. But I wanted more news of her than I got and was sad that even though we were physically closer, we were emotionally further apart.

In May 2018 she was arrested on three drug charges, including a class C felony. At that point, Darci finally sent me a text message. When we met up, she explained that officers had pulled her over after she failed to signal before turning off the road at Morrilton, about an hour away. They found Xanax and hydrocodone in her car. Virginia bailed her out. Over the next few months, Darci was arrested twice more for traffic infractions. She had been so happy to finally be finished with parole, and here she was again, facing more charges. The prosecutor in the drug case wanted to enhance the charges because she was a repeat offender. She stopped returning my calls and texts, but I knew she'd been evicted from her apartment.

Around this time, I met up with a friend of ours from high school, someone who didn't want me to use her name. The friend admitted to me, in confidence, that she snorted meth every morning as if it were a cup of coffee. She had since we were teenagers. It got her through the day, she said. "I don't want to know what's going on with my liver," she said, laughing. She said she couldn't function without it. But the important thing was that she did function. She kept her job, she stayed safe, and she took care of her daughter. She maintained close ties with her family and would be okay in life. Her use might be physically bad for her, but she didn't go through the repeated cycles that Darci did.

"That's what I want for Darci," I said, and caught her up on Darci's repeated problems. I thought Darci needed a way to use and still be safe. Advocates call this harm reduction: prioritizing keeping users alive rather than punishing them for their use. The problem with Darci was that she always went on a fast and desperate downward spiral at the first opportunity. I worried she'd end up in a gas station bathroom again, high or worse.

"Here's the thing," my friend said. "Maybe that's what Darci wants. I don't think Darci wants to be stable."

I thought about my own life, and I realized that this was what still pinned Darci and me together, the essential thing we still had in common, a connected part of our being. We shared a desire for a messy life. We both had a fear of being too settled, of being trapped.

Some people, maybe most people, find happiness in stability, a life contained in four walls and a roof, but Darci and I never had and never would. We'd always been different, and we'd been different together. We had the same unhealed wounds, and because of them, we could never be satisfied with being still. I had left Clinton and found constructive ways to channel that impulse. Darci stayed and tried to squeeze herself into its ill-fitting confines, and it had slowly destroyed her. Sometimes she would get high, she told me, and lie down in the middle of whatever busy road she was nearest. She wasn't trying to commit suicide, she said. She did it because nothing stopped her. I'm not sure the world has ever figured out how to handle the Darcis who live in it. Our hometown definitely had not.

. . .

Everyday life in Clinton was harder than Samir and I had expected. Services, from trash pickup to Internet, were more expensive and less reliable than we'd been used to in the D.C. suburbs. Shopping often meant, as it had in my youth, a nearly hour-long drive to Conway. But now downtown didn't have enough sidewalks, making it harder to walk around and casually see people. Such seemingly small things shifted the patterns of our everyday lives in unexpected ways and were far more isolating than we were used to.

Many of the town's problems were structural. Instead of repairing sidewalks and reinvesting in downtown, for instance, Clinton had banked on nearby highway retail to generate tax revenue and prop up the local economy. In 2017 Dollar General built a new building a couple of doors down from its old one, which stood empty. But other businesses along the highway closed down, leaving their empty steel husks decrepit. The old Walmart in town closed when a supercenter arrived farther south. A used furniture store filled the old Walmart space for a time, but it, too, closed in 2019. Now the hulking metal building stands empty in front of a parking lot sprouting weeds. The county judge, Dale James, elected in 2018, tried to court more national and regional chains to take up lots along the highway. But if it happens, it will only extend the desolation further into the future.

The first municipal service to disappear was the animal shelter, run jointly by the county and the city. Neither government had the money to contribute to its budget, which was a little more than $110,000 a year, including salaries for staff to run the shelter and an animal control officer. The county contracted with a small nonprofit that struggled to raise funds, and packs of feral dogs roamed through smaller towns like Shirley or ended up dead by the highway in Clinton. The sight of dead dogs, cats, and deer on the roadsides gave the county a neglected, apocalyptic feel. A few times Samir and I had called the highway department, at the city hall, when we saw an animal's body, only to be told it was no one's job to cart it away.

By 2019 the county was struggling to keep up with funding the library, the volunteer fire departments, and the hospital building, but voters rejected an extension of a penny sales tax that would have covered everything. The county government shrank, and jobs were cut. And still people said these services weren't the government's job, that they should be managed by the private sector or by individuals.

When faced with any disaster, the voting people of Van Buren County—the business owners, the church leaders, the middle class—largely doubled down on their conservatism, religiosity, and isolationism. (Darci, like many of the most desperate people, did not vote. Owing restitution for her crime, she was not allowed to register. She also wasn't eager to keep government updated on her whereabouts.) The charitable institutions that remained— from the food banks to the drug rehabilitation centers—were based in churches, outside state or federal oversight, so they could choose who they would and wouldn't serve.

The Republican county sheriff, Lucas Emberton, first elected in 2018, won on a platform of cracking down on drug users. Though a referendum had passed legalizing medical cannabis in the state, Emberton also promised to target people with marijuana, which he called a gateway drug. He said drug arrests were his priority. "People get involved with other things, opioids and marijuana," Emberton told the state paper, "and that one time they're vulnerable to a friend and they try it [methamphetamine], that is 98 percent addictive after the first time. . . . Our goal is to attack narcotics aggressively." Vanessa's mom, Susie, told a state television station that she hoped Emberton would be the Clint Eastwood of Van Buren County.

But to those most affected, the cycle of arrests was beside the point. "We have addicts that are doing whatever they can get, or taking whatever they can get, to get high," said Callie Davidson, the mother of a young woman who'd been swept up in a drug raid. "I think our response needs to be, let's rehabilitate these guys. The prison system is overflowing with addicts, but then there's no money for rehabs."

When the Covid-19 pandemic arrived, in March 2020, many people in Clinton were ready to downplay it. People died all the time, they said. "If the Good Lord is ready to take me, there's nothing I can do to stop it," the secretary of a local nondenominational church announced on Facebook. This was something I'd heard all my life. Many people in town were hostile to government closures.

Throughout the pandemic, a minority of us had real questions and concerns: Where were the infections occurring? What was the county doing to protect the vulnerable? What were the hospitals and nursing homes doing to control infection? Our community faced a problem that would be easiest for us to solve together, but its leaders instead counseled reliance on individual Christian faith—whether people were Christian or not. This translated into an idea that people shouldn't rely on the government, even at the local level. "Being a Republican, I agree with our platform which boldly states that we should exercise personal responsibility," the county judge, Dale James, announced on his Facebook page. This kind of message encouraged behavior that helped spread the virus. People ignored public health measures like mandates to wear face masks or get vaccinated unless they were worried about their own health. They saw it solely as a matter of personal choice when, in reality, masks and vaccines were also meant to protect the people around us. What almost no one talked about on Facebook, or anywhere else, was our responsibilities to each other. Less than half the population of Arkansas was vaccinated even into 2022, after the Delta and Omicron variants had swept through the state. In 2021 the Covid-19 death rate in rural America surpassed that of the rest of the country.

In the summer of 2020, many people in Clinton were more

frightened of Black Lives Matter protests, all of which were peaceful, around the state, than they were of Covid-19. The Ozarks are home to many hate groups, especially around the town of Harrison, but a few antiracism activists had sprung up around them, and even Harrison had a Black Lives Matter protest.

People in Clinton took to local news groups on Facebook to post about the protests. "Do y'all think protests will come through our town?" someone asked on one of the biggest local groups. Some replied that it was time to get out their guns. "Ain't nobody coming up here. They know the road to Harrison," that home of hate groups, said Jared Betnar, a Clinton local who helped moderate the Facebook group. Later, when Kyle Rittenhouse was arrested and charged with murdering protesters in Kenosha, Wisconsin, Clinton celebrated him as a hero, for doing what he had to do to protect property.

A few friends from town who lived elsewhere called out this racism. A friend of mine who lived in Conway called it "hillbilly hysteria." If it was, it was a familiar kind, the same kind that had been mobilized against Black towns across the South, from Reconstruction to the 1960s. Many Americans believe the land they've inherited, though initially stolen in the Native American genocide, is their birthright. Land and homes in rural Arkansas aren't worth much financially, but they offer the psychic relief of knowing you always have a piece of earth that belongs to you. W.E.B. Du Bois's "psychological wage" of whiteness, its title to the universe, took physical form in the land claimed by families here, a privilege denied Black Americans for centuries.

Property rights, land ownership, and gun ownership are all tied up in this political worldview. It doesn't matter to people in Clinton how destitute they are, how fundamentally poor the soil is, how frayed its social safety net. It doesn't matter that the antigovernment sentiment they espouse is heading to a nihilistic endpoint calling on the government to cut valuable programs they use themselves. Or that their outrage over taxation only helps the kind of wealthy people who don't live in Clinton. It doesn't matter to them that they have more in common with poor people of color than with rich white people. The white women in this community don't seem concerned that the systems they support shield their abusers and circumscribe their lives. Their inheritance came down to them as land, so that's what they want to protect. They concentrate on their own personal redemption, even as their communities are dying. It makes them withdraw from one another, ever further from a sense of community, so that people like Darci, who suffer the most, struggle to find anything safe to grab on to.

A study from the American Communities Project at the Michigan State University School of Journalism on rural counties published in 2019 found that the counties that are doing the best economically are those that welcome new immigrants. Immigrants open new businesses and inject local economies with much-needed energy. Counties that encourage artists to move in and build artistic communities also thrive. But Arkansans—and denizens of rural counties across the United States—vote and respond to national events in ways that are hostile to immigration, hostile to anyone from outside their own communities. They support presidents and senators and policies that would close the borders, cut taxes to nothing, and pass initiatives preventing schools from teaching about racism accurately. The 2021 legislative session in Arkansas passed legislation antagonistic to our changing world: it made abortion a felony in almost all cases, a law that was meant to challenge *Roe v. Wade* before that decision was struck down by the Supreme Court in 2022; it tried to prohibit teaching *The New York Times*'s "1619 Project," the Pulitzer Prize–winning journalism that examined the role of slavery in the country's founding, and the accurate history of our country's systemic racism; it banned gender-affirming healthcare for transgender youth; it even, ultimately, rejected federal funding for programs to help those who were unemployed or needed rental assistance during the pandemic. The new state laws were designed to pick a fight with the rest of the nation. Just as they had a century ago, people across rural America are choosing, in the face of change, to make their communities more insular, especially if it means keeping out people who don't look like them.

Many rural American counties face the dilemmas that Van Buren County does—the same decline in services, the same retreat from societal responsibilities—and have been largely left to deal with them on their own. In 2018 I visited a cluster of old coal towns in Kentucky, built in a narrow valley at the turn of the last century. In the 1970s the coal companies abandoned the area for bigger and cheaper strip-mining operations elsewhere, leaving most of the towns vacant. The people left behind are still trying to decide how to survive, what to do with their towns, and how to re-create an economy that will give them hope for a future. The mayor of one of these towns—John Adams of Lynch, Kentucky—told me that he thought the future of his town might be a retreat into the past. "Worst-case scenario, it goes back like it was a hundred years ago," he said. "A few families living here and there."

Was that what I was witnessing in Clinton, a slow unwinding of progress, a retrenchment back into nature? But residents of big cities that had lost their industrial base were experiencing a similar sense of loss and despair—blocks full of empty houses, the lack of basic services, the feeling that they were losing a battle with an earth that was ready to overtake them, to fold them back into the ground. Maybe that's what so many of these ill-gotten places, established in war and robbery, deserved. But those who suffered the most from this diminishment were never those who had benefited from the status quo ante. The people who had done the sowing didn't stick around to reap. Instead, it was the most vulnerable people whose lives were upended. In my society, it is those who don't fit neatly into the common conception of a proper life—especially the poorest women, squeezed between expectation and reality—who suffer the most.

• • •

The way Clinton approached the pandemic—passively accepting it, refusing to listen to science—helped me understand how they'd approached the drug epidemic that had preceded, and was likely to continue after, Covid-19. I saw it play out on a small scale in Darci's life.

On August 1, 2018, Darci was scheduled to appear in court in Morrilton to face drug charges. Virginia was frantic, worried that Darci would miss her date and Virginia would lose the bond she'd paid. Virginia asked me to pick Darci up at the Green Forest rehab the day before court, bring her back to Clinton, stay the night at Virginia's, and then take them both to court the next day.

When I arrived in Green Forest to pick her up, I expected Darci to be ready, but she was still half clothed and her hair was a mess. She'd been crying. Two men were in her apartment, neither of whom I'd met. One was in the kitchen making bacon and eggs that filled the room with the smell of grease and hot meat. The other, who I learned was her boyfriend, Jeremy, was pacing and yelling at Darci while she yelled nonsensically back at him.

Darci had been in jail for a couple of nights on a reckless driving charge and had just returned to her apartment the day before. Her car was still impounded. Since she'd been charged in Morrilton on drug possession, she'd picked up several other misdemeanors, mostly resulting from car stops around the state. It was a sign—worrying to me, to anyone paying attention—that she was losing control, that things were getting worse. I'd known that, watching from a distance, but here it was up close, in her crowded apartment.

I asked her if she was ready for her court date the next day.

"I guess I'm just not even going to go!" she said, crying. "They can put me as a no-show and put me in jail."

Jeremy came up to me, put his face close to mine, and jabbered, trying to convince me to get her car out of impound for $300. The smells, the screaming, Jeremy's uninvited closeness, and the general distress set me on edge. Even the calmness of the man cooking in the kitchen felt quietly menacing. The room lights were off, the TV was playing silently, flashing a bluish light around the room, and clothes were strewn everywhere across the floor.

Darci was still crying and increasingly angry, walking around in a near panic. I felt strongly that she needed to get out of there, and I said so. She wanted me to take her to a doctor's office in another town. I didn't know another way to get her to leave, so I said quickly, "I'll take you to the doctor, but we have to leave right now."

Once we were on the road, she calmed down. I asked her who the people in her apartment were and why they were there, but it all came out in a jumble. The man who had been cooking was the one who bailed Darci out from her arrest in Harrison, and I didn't know why or what he'd gotten in return. "I think he's in love with me," Darci said, and shrugged. But Jeremy was her boyfriend. I didn't try to untangle it, and Darci just stared out the window at a bright blue sky, framed by the green of the mountains we drove through.

At the doctor's office, Darci complained of a broken rib. They took an X-ray, and whatever they saw was enough to convince them that she needed hydrocodone, an opiate painkiller. She left with prescriptions for that and for her blood pressure medication, atenolol, a beta-blocker she often took. When I saw her emerge with the prescriptions, I knew I would not help her fill them. I wasn't going to judge her, in that moment, for her drug use, but I also wasn't going to buy the drugs for her. I told her I didn't want to stop in the rain and dropped her off at her mother's house.

Early the next morning Virginia and Darci met me in a parking lot across from my house, to drive them to court. I drove her car, which had more room than mine. Darci's appearance before the judge was brief: she filled out a form to be assigned a court-appointed attorney. The public defender glanced at her application, agreed to represent her, asked for a new court date, and we left. The courtroom was filled with people who'd gone through a similar process, facing similar charges.

On the drive back to Clinton afterward, Darci mentioned the prescriptions again. She was a font of constant chatter, mostly about her health. She was on Medicaid, which allowed only four prescriptions to be filled in a month. The rest she'd have to pay cash for. She kept doing the math—obsessively and eagerly, drumming her fingers against her knee, as if she were counting—while Virginia sat, mostly silent, in the back seat.

Finally, Virginia said. "Well, the thing is, I don't have the money to pay for all this stuff." This was probably true, but everyone in the car knew it wasn't about the money. Virginia didn't want Darci to have hydrocodone while she was in her house.

This made Darci angry, so she needled Virginia about how she was raising Maddie. "Where does Maddie get the money for her vape stuff?" she asked, an angry edge to her voice.

Virginia, taken aback, told Darci that she and David had spoken to Maddie about not vaping and thought she'd stopped; Darci said all the evidence was in plain sight in Maddie's room, and she grew increasingly upset that Virginia hadn't seen it. She screamed and turned to me. "My children are not safe with them," she said, pointing at her mom. "My fifteen-year-old daughter smokes. You should hear the things she says, because she's honest with me." Then she focused on Virginia again. "You and David are a joke to them because they know they can get whatever they want and do whatever they want"—her voice breaking, choking, shrieking— "just like I did."

I paid close attention to the road, my heart beating faster and faster, because what seemed to be unfolding in the car was, in microcosm, the story of Darci's life. All the fights that she and Virginia had ever had, the tensions and disappointments beneath their relationship, were here, at the surface.

Darci bent over, whining in agony, clutching her stomach, and I knew her pain was both physical and emotional. The sound she made then—guttural and wretched—will stay with me forever. I felt guilty—I knew her pain was real. She wanted the hydrocodone for it, and I'd played a part in preventing her from getting it. I felt guilty for not visiting her in the previous weeks. When she'd stopped reaching out to me, I'd thought she'd wanted space, and I hadn't driven the two hours to see her because I thought she wouldn't be home or free to visit with me. But she'd filled the space I'd given her with men, drugs, and a summer of petty crime. I also felt guilty for bringing her back to Clinton. Not only because it precipitated this toxic fight but because something about just being in Clinton had always been hard on her. People in my hometown always ask me if I was scared or nervous to live in New York and D.C. What I felt acutely in that car was that the worst things that had ever happened to me or to Darci had happened here, just a few miles from where we were born.

Darci asked me to stop the car, but I kept driving, determined to get somewhere safe. There was construction on the highway; workers milled about on the shoulder amid the orange cones, and the heavy traffic squeezed into the open lanes. I felt bound to deliver them both home safely or at least somewhere calmer.

But Darci kept begging me to stop, over and over. I told her to take a deep breath and then locked the doors. That made it worse. "I'm really about to freak the fuck out!" she screamed, trying to open the door, threatening to jump out while the car was moving. And then she moaned and clutched her stomach again.

I turned off of the highway and slowed down as we arrived in Clinton. I had no idea what to do. I had meant to return to the parking lot where we'd met that morning, to get out there and let Virginia drive her car home. But I was worried about Darci and suddenly didn't want her and Virginia going home together alone.

"Do you want to go to the hospital?" I asked Virginia, who knew I was asking whether she wanted me to take Darci to the hospital. "I don't know," she said.

I turned into the parking lot, thinking we might double back toward the hospital when I heard a click and several pings. Then I heard Darci scream, "You bitch!"

I heard Virginia's sharp intake of breath and saw Darci's empty seat. She'd jumped out after all and rolled behind the car. I looked in the rearview mirror and saw her get up from the asphalt, pull down her skirt, and rub her thigh as she marched angrily away toward the grocery store at the other end of the parking lot. I put the car in park and sat there, watching her walk away, the turn signal clicking.

"What should we do?" I asked Virginia. She said we should just go home.

This was what it had always felt like to be Darci's friend: unsure and unsettled. It had seemed good when we were kids wanting adventure, but now it felt mostly bad.

I didn't see or speak to Darci for several months after she

jumped out of the car, and I wasn't eager to: I was upset by what had happened and wanted to keep my distance. The next time I saw Virginia, I told her she might be able to convince a judge that Darci needed to be hospitalized for a mental health screening. Doctors and hospitals hadn't always been good for Darci, but being hospitalized might keep her safe and allow her to get help.

Virginia just raised her hands and said, as she had many times before, "I don't know what to do."

• • •

I loved the little house that Samir and I had rented. It had a creaky wooden wraparound porch and a pokeweed-covered yard. It was old and rickety and precarious, hugging the rocky hillside. It looked like it might slide down the hill at any moment, but it was solid, a survivor. Added on to and patched up over the years, it was probably one of the oldest houses in town and had once belonged to a man who'd been mayor and sheriff. It stood on the corner of two streets that no longer existed but had been drawn on old maps and in the real world had cracked apart. The property was fenced in by big oak trees. Often when I told people where I lived, even people who'd lived in Clinton their whole lives would say, "There's a house up there?" From my porch I could see much of downtown—the stores, the Pizza Hut, the giant American flag that waved in front of the bank, the cars pulsing down the highway all day. It almost seemed not to belong in Clinton; it was also exactly like the town to forget a house that had been standing at its center from its earliest days.

Darci had visited only once, and when I gave her a tour, she picked up on these qualities too. "I love it, Monica," she'd said and laughed. Then she joked about being there at night, watching the cars drive on the highway. "Do you know how many tweakers would love this? Sitting on the porch, being high, and watching all these lights?"

• • •

Darci's downward spiral continued into the summer and fall. She stopped going to court appearances. By then she had pending charges in three counties, the most severe for the drug arrest in Morrilton. When she failed to appear for her subsequent court dates on those charges, a warrant was issued for her arrest. In February 2019, four months after I'd last seen her, a bail bonds-man arrived at the run-down motel-turned-apartment where she was staying, arrested her, and took her to jail.

A few weeks later I drove two hours to visit her at the county jail in Berryville. That morning was frosty and cold, and a thin sheet of ice covered the trees and grass and mountainsides, twin-kling and clear and white like a snow globe. In the visitors' room, we had to speak through phones on opposite sides of a bullet-proof partition. She wore an orange jumpsuit and had the same washed-out look as the women around her, as if she'd been scrubbed with salt and sandpaper. The hair beneath her ponytail had been shaved, and she was very thin. She told me she and Jer-emy had both been arrested, and that they'd been using meth for a full year. Meth hadn't been Darci's drug of choice in the past, but during this period of her life, it had consumed her. She wanted meth more than she wanted food, and meth was often free.

Our visit was short, just the allotted fifteen minutes. Soon af-terward Darci was transferred to the county jail in Morrilton. She pleaded guilty to the drug charges, and her court-appointed at-torney asked for leniency and a sentence of five years' probation. "She did good for so long," he told the presiding judge, and I wondered quietly, *On what planet has Darci been doing well?* But it had been several years since she'd gotten a felony charge. The court was designed to see crimes, not suffering, not the cycle of despair in which Darci lived. She got probation.

When I picked her up from jail, she rushed out in the tank top, shorts, and flip-flops she'd been arrested in. I asked how long she had been inside, total. "One hundred and three days," she said. On the way back to Clinton, she complained about the food she'd had while incarcerated. All she'd eaten for months was hot dogs and bologna. Her stomach hurt, and she had a particular pain in her side. I told her it was probably just the food. I dropped her off at Virginia and David's house.

Virginia called me the next morning. Darci had been in severe pain throughout the night. At first, she and David hadn't believed her complaint—it seemed like drug-seeking behavior. Darci had just gotten home from jail, and she already wanted to go to the emergency room? But when Virginia pressed on her stomach, she'd seen real pain in Darci's face. At the emergency room at our local hospital, the doctor diagnosed her with acute appendicitis. They transferred her by ambulance to the bigger hospital in Conway, where she was likely to get into surgery faster.

Virginia and I went to the hospital the next morning. The surgeon told us her appendix had already ruptured, but she was lucky because the infected tissue had stayed in one place, trapped by the organs around her appendix, unable to invade the rest of her body. She was honest about her drug-use history, but she was also in a lot of pain. "You were really sick," he said, nodding.

I felt immense relief that Darci had been home that night. If she'd still been in jail, the officers wouldn't have believed she was in pain. She could have died there.

Darci's weeklong stay in the hospital put her in a contemplative mood. A week or so after she was released, we went to Sonic to get ice cream. She was trying to decide whether to return to Dorcas House. Again, she had begged them to give her another chance, and, again, they had agreed. She was scheduled to go the next day. But she'd just found out that Virginia was in legal trouble herself. The water department where she'd worked for more than thirty years, in Bee Branch, had accused her of embezzling about $173,000. It was a crime almost like Darci's at Ferrellgas, but it had unfolded over four years of doctoring books to hide the stolen money. According to police records, after she was confronted, she told the investigators that she was glad it was over with. Most of the money, she later told me, had gone to pay bills. She would ultimately plead guilty and was sentenced to a suspended prison term of twenty years, which meant that she was on unsupervised probation. If she failed to follow the terms of her probation, including paying restitution, the suspension of her sentence could be revoked, and she would finish her term in prison.

Without Virginia working, relying only on David's Social Security and help from food banks and other programs, money would be tight. Darci told me, on the way home from Sonic, that she might be able to help her mom by getting a job. I told Darci the best way to help her mom and her family was to work on herself, to get sober and be more stable. Darci started to cry. "Mom went to a place I never thought she'd go," she said. "She said that if George and I had it together, she wouldn't have stolen the money." She cried for a while, looking out my windshield. Then I took her home.

She didn't return to Dorcas House the next day, or ever, and she didn't stay home to help her mom. But she got clean. During a meeting with her probation officer, she complained about being unable to see a therapist or to receive any mental health medications because of changes in her Medicaid plan. The officer mentioned that she could check herself into a behavioral health hospital if she felt she needed to.

It surprised me that Darci followed this advice, but over the next two months, she sought care in two different hospitals. After her second stay, at a hospital in Fayetteville, she was entered into a buprenorphine clinic, which would enable her to receive medication and participate in group therapy sessions for two years. Buprenorphines, a class of drugs that includes the brand name Suboxone, have shown success in preventing overdoses, death, and other problems associated with drug addiction. It can be difficult to get because, in many states, doctors have to enroll in a special licensing program to be able to prescribe it, but advocates and researchers have long touted its success.

Darci returned to Clinton at the end of 2019. She said that with Suboxone she could control her cravings without getting high. She'd tried to get high, she told me, but it had just made her sick. She didn't want to anymore.

We started walking in the park again. One day she was really upset about a friend who had committed suicide. She had known he took pills and drank, but he and his wife always seemed like a happy couple, and he was a good guy. "I can almost understand the head space he was in," Darci said. "When you take a lot of benzos and drink a lot, which he did, you can go down down down down down. It can make something that isn't sensible seem sensible."

I thought about the quietness of Darci's statement, and the solitude of her depression. I thought about her long history of unacknowledged pain set against the backdrop of the chaos throughout our world. The stories of our lives and our town were tiny in comparison, really, but we were buffeted by the same forces that troubled the entire country. Places like my hometown are still romanticized as the American heartland, but the reality of life in those towns drifts further from that idyll every year. If we don't reckon with this disparity, rural America won't be able to break out of the cycle of despair.

. . .

From 2019 to 2022, Darci seemed really sober. Her probation officer required her to get a job, and instead of fighting about it, she just went out and got one at a gas station in Choctaw. It was the same gas station where Vanessa had found her bloody and beaten four years before, the same one she'd been in when the paramedics arrived to take her to the hospital. Her main job there was serving fried chicken.

After the pandemic struck, Darci and I had a hard time meeting up, mostly because she always seemed busy. We checked in with each other, though. She told me that she, her mom, and her stepdad were all getting along. She worked a lot, and when she came home, she either slept or cleaned her house. Her life was boring, she said—which was just what I had hoped it would be.

What part of the cycle are we in now? That's what I wondered most often. Was this just a long, slow period after her last institutionalization and before her next decline? Was her treatment just delaying the inevitable?

One day after we first reconnected in the spring of 2015, Darci and I had lunch at a ministry downtown, in an old storefront. It served meals there every day, asking that diners pay whatever they could afford. (Diners could eat for free if they agreed to have a private chat with the minister.) We had something called chicken spaghetti, but Darci barely ate. She was on the edge of her seat, saying hi to everyone she knew, running her fork through her food, and getting distracted.

She knew I wanted to write about our lives and our hometown. She and I had been talking about our childhood and our time apart, but she had done more talking than I had. I told her she could ask me anything she wanted.

"So many questions!" she had said, but couldn't quite form them before she got distracted again. "So many questions!"

I wanted her to ask me about my life, about anything, to let me tell a story the way she'd been telling hers to me. I wanted her to be curious about what I'd done and why, and why I'd been coming back home—I wanted her to seek a connection with me. But she never asked me anything like that. Instead, she talked, distractedly, about herself.

She'd had a hysterectomy that spring, and she told me she was feeling weird because of the hormones she'd been taking afterward. "I'm not high, I promise!" She put her hands over her face, basically confirming that she was. She threw her arms up in a V. "I feel like 'Towanda!'" she said, quoting from *Fried Green Tomatoes,* one of our favorite movies when we were kids.

"Oh, wait, I do have a question!" Darci finally said. "At the end of this book, will they know we're best friends?"

I thought about that a lot over the next few years, when Darci was away and when she was home, when she was doing badly and when she was doing better. I thought about it most when we were apart. What did that term *best friends* really mean for adults who had spent most of their lives apart? We didn't see each other regularly, and whenever we did, there was a crisis. We didn't have the push and pull of best friends, nor the honest conversations. We didn't read the same books or watch the same movies, and when she was in prison, we had trouble communicating at all. Virginia wanted me to help take care of her during her roughest times, but those were the times when Darci avoided me—as I had sometimes avoided her, to save myself frustration and pain.

Yet I knew I'd never had a better friend than Darci, not one with that same uncomplicated closeness. Maybe I'd held that spot open for Darci, should she ever wish to occupy it again, holding myself back from allowing anyone else to take it. We were friends because we had once been friends, because the strong connections young children forge can stay locked in place forever. Your life bends around the shape of that bond, keeping it intact. Darci knew my deepest wounds. She knew that everything I'd done and was doing was, in some way, because I'd lost Ashley and buried her in Clinton, and I knew that about her too. That grief, and the larger, shared understanding of growing up where we had and wanting to get out, would always fill whatever space might grow between us.

ACKNOWLEDGMENTS

I'd like to start by thanking my editors at *The American Prospect*, especially Ann Friedman and Mark Schmitt, who hired me when I was a newspaper reporter and helped turn me into a magazine writer, and Kit Rachlis, whose mentorship helped me become an even better writer. The folks at New America, especially Reid Cramer and Anne-Marie Slaughter, supported my work early on, and I wouldn't have been able to write a book at all without their fellowship support.

A huge thanks to Elyse Cheney at The Cheney Agency for making this book possible, and for all of her and Adam Eaglin's support and guidance over the years; this book wouldn't exist without them. Immeasurable thanks also to my editors at Penguin Random House—Robin Desser for her guidance and patience, Hilary Redmon for her insights and help bringing it home, and Helen Conford and Casiana Ionita in the U.K. Also, a special thanks to Tangela Mitchell, Claire Wang, Hayden Mora, and Miriam Khanukaev.

Thanks to Darci for being my friend through the years and for trusting me with her life story. Thanks to everyone who agreed to talk to me for this book, and to the state of Arkansas, for being such a challenging, confounding, and beautiful muse.

My colleagues—in graduate school, during my early days as a newspaper clerk, while blogging with the PostBourgie crew, over dinners discussing longform journalism at Kit's house, and up until today working at FiveThirtyEight—have informed my journalism in one way or another and always made it better.

My mom has supported me in every way possible throughout my life and I'll never be able to fully repay her in gratitude, but I will try. Special thanks to each and every friend who has supported me in this endeavor, especially Nicole and the chateau. Thanks also to Courtney and Sean for being family. And a huge thanks to Samir, the love of my life, who witnessed the darkest days and helped bring me through them, and who now knows what it's like to go through the huge challenge of writing a book and who deserves some of the credit for this one making it out into the world at all.

Monica Potts is a senior politics reporter for the web-site FiveThirtyEight. Her previous work has appeared in *The New York Times, The Atlantic,* and *The New Republic,* among other publications, and on NPR. She was a 2015–16 New America Fellow and is a former senior writer with *The American Prospect.* She lives in central New York.

monicapotts.com

ABOUT THE TYPE

This book was set in Sabon, a typeface designed by the well-known German typographer Jan Tschichold (1902–74). Sabon's design is based upon the original letterforms of sixteenth-century French type designer Claude Garamond and was created specifically to be used for three sources: foundry type for hand composition, Linotype, and Monotype. Tschichold named his typeface for the famous Frankfurt typefounder Jacques Sabon (c. 1520–80).